My Grandfather's Clocks

GREGORY GERARD ALLISON

Name: Allison, Gregory Gerard, author
Title: My Grandfather's Clocks: a grandson's search for an American inventor's lost collection | Gregory Gerard Allison
Description: First U.S. edition (GRC61) | The Big Brick Review
Identifiers: ISBN 979-8-9907812-1-4 (paperback, black and white)
Subjects: Biography & memoir | Watchmaking in the 20th century | American inventors
Cover design: Eric Wilder
Author photo: Sonja Livingston
Photography: Pre-1999 images from Allison family archives
Photography: Post-2000 images by Gregory Gerard Allison

First U.S. Edition: 2024
For more information, visit www.CharlesAllisonClocks.com

DEDICATION

This book is dedicated to my newly discovered stepcousin
Judy Allison (of Montana)
whose generosity, kindness, and tenacity in solving mysteries
have helped me see that there is still great goodness to be found in this world.

CONTENTS

CHARLES ALLISON FAMILY TREE

FIRST MARRIAGE

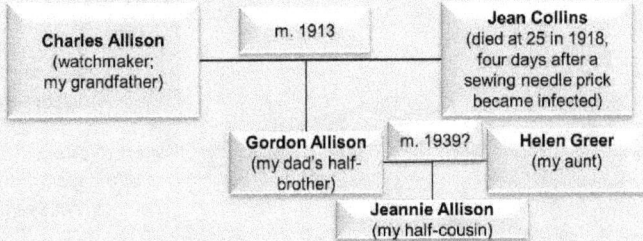

| Charles Allison (watchmaker; my grandfather) | m. 1913 | Jean Collins (died at 25 in 1918, four days after a sewing needle prick became infected) |

Gordon Allison (my dad's half-brother) — m. 1939? — Helen Greer (my aunt)

Jeannie Allison (my half-cousin)

SECOND MARRIAGE

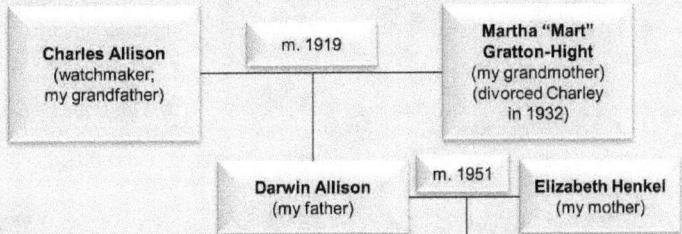

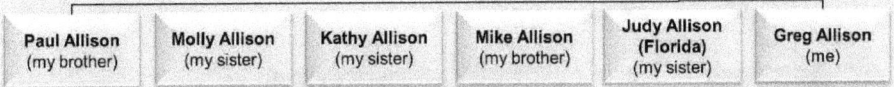

| Charles Allison (watchmaker; my grandfather) | m. 1919 | Martha "Mart" Gratton-Hight (my grandmother) (divorced Charley in 1932) |

Darwin Allison (my father) — m. 1951 — Elizabeth Henkel (my mother)

| Paul Allison (my brother) | Molly Allison (my sister) | Kathy Allison (my sister) | Mike Allison (my brother) | Judy Allison (Florida) (my sister) | Greg Allison (me) |

THIRD MARRIAGE

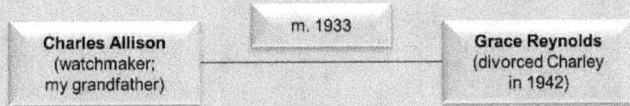

| Charles Allison (watchmaker; my grandfather) | m. 1933 | Grace Reynolds (divorced Charley in 1942) |

FOURTH MARRIAGE

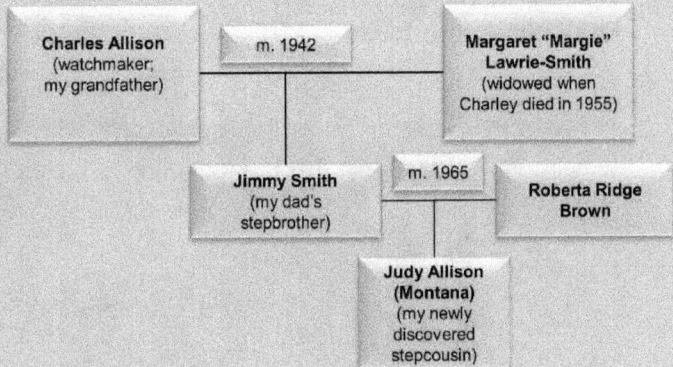

| Charles Allison (watchmaker; my grandfather) | m. 1942 | Margaret "Margie" Lawrie-Smith (widowed when Charley died in 1955) |

Jimmy Smith (my dad's stepbrother) — m. 1965 — Roberta Ridge Brown

Judy Allison (Montana) (my newly discovered stepcousin)

The Charles Allison Timepiece Collection
(1936 – 1952)

1936
(est)

Allison Watchmakers' Visitors Book comments

'Significant simplicity with true craftsmanship. One of the world's wonders.'
—Mrs. Lyman Moore, Washington, DC

'Four generations of jewelers never saw anything like this.'
—Louis Keirtt, Buffalo, NY

'The most incredible and wonderful [clocks] that I have ever seen.'
—Mary van der Winde, East Kent, England

'Now I believe in magic.'
—Ruth Bradley, Venice, CA

1937 (est)

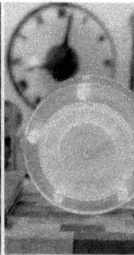

1938 (est)

1939 (est)

1940

1941

1943 (est)

1944

1945 (est)

1946 (est)

1948 (est)

1950 (est)

1952

To the reader:

I encountered many people in my travels to solve this mystery. Where I've changed names to respect others' privacy, I've indicated that I renamed them.

As you'll learn in the coming pages, I've worked hard to uncover the details of my grandfather's life and relate them for you in an accurate, digestible, chronological format. In some cases, I have letters, photographs, and official records, which give me actual dates, times, and details. These facts I'm sure of.

In other cases, I've heard about my grandfather through the oral history of my family—from my grandmother, from my uncle, from my father and mother, and from my siblings. Some of these stories have been confirmed by records I've uncovered; for others, there are simply no records to corroborate what I've heard. That said, I believe them all to be reasonably reliable—and I've called those details out as 'family lore.'

Finally, just based on the immensity of my research into my grandfather's life (including the physical clocks themselves, their innovations, and, in some cases, corrected flaws), I have gained a sense of who he was and what might have motivated him. In those cases, I've called out my speculations using words like 'probably' or 'most likely.'

Believe me, I couldn't make this stuff up if I tried.

–Gregory Gerard Allison
Spring 2024

Time is the wisest of all things that are,
    for it brings everything to light.
                        –Thales, Greek philosopher

PROLOGUE

Summer 1975

The clock is about six inches tall, but it's hard to know for sure because it's under a glass dome. It's on one of the upper shelves in our home library, out of my nine-year-old reach. The clock has been there as long as I can remember.

I know a few things about it. It's old. My grandfather, Charles Allison, made it. My dad, Darwin Allison, broke it.

With the Western New York skies serving up sheets of rain to drench the grassy acres surrounding our brick farmhouse, I'm looking for indoor ways to break the boredom. This afternoon, the clock has grabbed my attention.

I pull the ottoman away from the library's reading chair and position it next to the shelves. We don't actually read in here—my dad's baby grand piano fills a good chunk of the room and, with east-facing windows and cherry-wood paneling, it's one of the darkest rooms in the house.

Climbing up, I turn on the flashlight I've retrieved from the cubby hole in the laundry room. I stare at the clock, trying to act like one of the Hardy Boys or Nancy Drew examining an important clue.

It's a miniature grandfather model. The case is a dull silver metal, with a rounded top and pedestal base. A brass-colored pendulum and chimes hang down the middle.

The hands on the brass face of the clock are stuck on the two and the ten. They never move—and I know why. Family stories have told me that my genius grandfather gave this clock to my left-handed dad as a wedding gift. Without any instructions, my dad accidentally wound it the wrong way—right-handed—on the very first turn.

The clock broke in 1953. Shame has kept it broken.

I wonder if this is part of the reason my dad gets mad so much.

Mom has told me a few things about my father's childhood. That his own dad, the watchmaker, left New York for California when my dad was twelve, right after the divorce from my grandmother. That my dad began playing piano in an East Rochester bar two years later, right after Prohibition ended. That he started drinking around the same time.

I train the flashlight on the little clock's face. Tiny letters spell out 'ALLISON' in fancy script behind the clock's hands. My last name. *Cool.*

At the bottom, there is a tented note card, like you see in school trophy cases. On the side facing me, I recognize my father's printing and reread the familiar note:

SEE IF YOU CAN FIND ONE LIKE THIS. LOVE, DAD

I read it again and think it through. Why would my father write this note in his own wedding gift? It doesn't make any sense.

Finishing my examination, I put the ottoman and flashlight back, then head to the kitchen. My mom is there, making a Saturday afternoon batch of fudge to raise our spirits on this gloomy day. As the youngest, I often get to scrape leftovers out of the pan after she doles the finished product onto a platter.

Mom is often trying to lose weight—sometimes successfully, sometimes not. Today, her girth blocks much of the stove. Flecks of gray have recently begun to pepper her thick, dark locks. I stand at her hip and wait.

"How come Dad wrote a note in the broken clock that says 'See if you can find one like this?'" I ask, my eyes focused on the fudge mixture as she churns. When it reaches the soft-ball stage, it's ready to pour. My stomach growls.

Mom laughs. "Honey, your dad didn't write that. That's Grandpa Charley's note to your dad when he shipped us the clock."

I take this in, hardly believing that my father's and my grandfather's handwriting can be so alike. I mean the note really looks like my dad wrote it.

"Oh," I say, keeping my gaze locked firmly on the fudge. As my eyes watch the brown mixture bubble, my mind crawls over the mysteries of ancestry and DNA. My own handwriting looks nothing like my father's.

My dad is left-handed and I am right-handed. But that's only the beginning of the gulf that divides us. At six feet and 250 pounds, he seems to plow through his days as a big, angry force, glossing over details in his wake, swearing (and sometimes ranting) at life's bumps.

The very opposite of me. I want to be a detective when I grow up. Details are my bread and butter. If I find old pictures in one of our many attic boxes, I always check the backs for names and dates. When I read a Hardy Boys story, I mentally catalogue the clues to try and figure out the mystery.

And I'm pretty even-tempered. I always try to make everybody happy.

If only I had been there to help wind my grandfather's special clock that first time, maybe I could have paid more attention and it wouldn't have broken. Maybe then my dad would have had a closer relationship with his dad.

And, if all of that had happened, maybe then my father would be more like the dads on TV, who play ball with their sons and take them fishing and hug them when life gets tough.

PART ONE
CLUES

G

GREG'S STORY

(1981 – 2018)

CHAPTER 1

September 1981

"He was a millionaire," my father says, taking a dramatic pause to drag on his cigarette and sip at his scotch. "With a big hat and a Texas drawl. An oil man."

Dad is drinking, so this will be longwinded. We sit around the blackened oak table in our kitchen. My sturdy wooden chair creaks as I shift for comfort. Since the onset of adolescence, the inevitability of DNA has added more than thirty pounds to my growing frame. A lot of it around my middle.

I don't usually like hanging around my dad when he's drinking—he becomes a verbose professor. For that matter, I don't usually like hanging around my dad when he's sober—his daytime, grocery-store-owner persona often barks commands at whichever of his six children is assigned to work that day.

But tonight is different. My father is telling family history, from back when FDR and JFK were alive and my ancestors fought in wars, performed music, and built things.

Tonight, the topic is clocks.

"The Oil Man had become aware of the shop—your grandfather had built quite a reputation for excellence in the Los Angeles arena." Big words. Drinking Dad always uses formal speak. "Allison Watchmakers attracted curiosity seekers from nearby Santa Monica, Beverly Hills, and Hollywood."

My dad pauses again, this time to wipe the back of his left hand across his lips. He always does this when he's drinking. I have no idea why.

"So, like many in town, he came out to view my father's collection. There were thirteen clocks in total. They weren't for sale. My father earned a living repairing watches, but he made clocks just to see what he could create. Although, technically, his creations were also considered watches." Drinking Dad slips easily into 'lecture mode.'

His grayish hair is puffed out a little bit on the sides, like college professors you might see in an old Sherlock Holmes movie—the chubby kind with a pipe and thick eyebrows.

"Do you know the difference between a watch and a clock?" he asks, waiting for my answer as he blows cigarette smoke toward the family room. Given my roots, I feel like I should know things like this. But, as the youngest in our family, I've learned not to ask about what I don't know. Quiet is safer than stupid.

"You wear a watch on your wrist?" I guess, raising my eyebrows to try and look knowledgeable.

My father chuckles. "Everyone makes that mistake. No, a clock is distinguished from a watch by the presence of a pendulum. If it has no pendulum, it is a watch—even if it hangs on the wall."

I nod and purse my lips as if this is not news to me.

"So the Texas Oil Man was impressed with my father's most unique creation: the Allison Mystery Watch." He leans forward, setting his scotch tumbler off its coaster. My dad doesn't pay much attention to details like this, just one more thing I can't relate to.

"The Mystery Watch was fastened to a flat square of wood—two feet by two feet." Drinking Dad gestures with his right hand, his cigarette dropping a few stray ashes as he makes a circle. "It had all the numbers of a clock-face, one through twelve, but there were no guts to it—no gears, no mechanics, no works." He looks directly at me now, but his eyes are seeing something else. My grandfather's shop, I guess, way off on the other side of the country from Western New York. I sense the awe my father has for my grandfather, a man he barely knew.

When my dad was twelve, my grandparents divorced—a huge shame in 1932. My mom told me privately that it really hurt my dad, having to choose whether to stay with his mom in New York or go with his dad and half-brother to California.

"He doesn't really know how to be a dad because his own dad left," she'd say, in the tone she uses to make excuses for his angry tantrums that often erupt in our household. But never when he is drinking. Drinking Dad is as pleasant as Mr. Rogers.

"The Mystery Watch had two wooden hands on it to indicate the time. They spun freely on a peg at the center of the clock. You could spin them around very fast and they would always come back to the correct time."

A thin smile breaks across my dad's lips. "My father thought of the design in a dream." He hasn't shifted his gaze, but now I feel that he's seeing me. "That's true genius, Son." He sets the tumbler on the table again and wipes his hand across his lips.

"He once told me the only way that clock would stop telling the correct time was if the earth fell off its axis. He made a smaller version on a similar principle, which he called the American Mystery Watch."

My chest expands with the thought of it. *A genius grandfather.* I think this might be where I got my good memory from—in school, I can memorize facts quickly. And I'm good at figuring things out, like when I repurposed my cassette tape recorder to design a house-to-Greg communication system into my detective agency in our barn.

My father's smile increases. "So, on this particular occasion, the Texas Oil Man observed the Mystery Watch and said, 'That's the darndest thing I've ever seen! How much do y'all want for it, Allison?'" My dad adds a southern accent for the Oil Man's voice.

"Your grandfather looked at him and said, 'it's not for sale.'" My dad leans in. "My father was not a man who ever let anyone tell him what to do." The pride in his voice is palpable.

"So the Oil Man says, 'I want that clock! I'll give you a thousand dollars for it.'" I like where this is going.

"And, once again, my dad says, 'it's not for sale.'"

I swirl the straw in my glass of late-summer lemonade. Real stories are sometimes as good as—and sometimes better than—made-up ones.

"They went back and forth a bit and the Oil Man got so angry, he finally threw down a blank check and said, 'You fill out *any amount!* I want that clock!'"

He pauses, as much to sip his scotch as to add emphasis.

"And your grandfather replied, 'It's. Not. For. Sale.'"

My mind spins around these details—a blank check from a millionaire! A clock—*I mean a watch*—that worked without explanation! It's like something from a Stephen King story.

I ask the obvious question. "Where are all the clocks now?"

My father looks away.

"You're familiar with the one on our library shelf." I nod. "It was a wedding gift from my father," he says.

He pauses for the briefest of moments. The fact that he broke it on its first wind floats unspoken between us.

My father continues. "The rest of my father's clocks were supposed to go to a museum upon his death..." He exhales more smoke before he finishes the thought. "...but I don't know their ultimate disposition."

As my father takes a break to refill his tumbler, I use the opportunity to excuse myself. Heading upstairs, my mind continues to sift through the details of this exciting family story. I pull out my journal and record the facts.

I close the page with a vow: to locate my genius grandfather's missing collection someday—and maybe even solve the mystery of the Allison Mystery Watch.

CHAPTER 2

January 2003

Many years have passed since my fifteen-year-old vow. At 82, after a short period of decline, my father passed away peacefully in hospice care. He stopped drinking in his later years and a sweet, sober persona emerged. As his life wound down without the influence of alcohol, he told stories freely: some about his time in World War II, some about his father's clocks.

I inherit two artifacts in the Allison clock legacy: Charley's shop guest book and the broken miniature grandfather clock (I've long since given up calling Grandpa's creations 'watches'—people just look at you weird). The first I put in my fire safe and the second I place on a bookshelf in my own home, under the same glass dome from my childhood.

When friends come over, I occasionally tell Charley's story: the left-handed wind, the Texas Oil Man, the missing collection—all of it. The clock continues its broken vigil as the responsibilities of family and work keep my days filled.

December 2017

Having entered my fifties, I am enjoying a holiday break from my daytime job (IT communications/proposal management) and my spare-time job (writing/teaching). Winter gusts shake my Rochester, NY Victorian home as snow swirls past the windows. Sitting in front of our third-floor woodstove, I sip a cocktail and reflect.

Entering a new decade (fifties!) is a great time to draw lines across the maps of our lives—the calendar's way of nudging us to review where we've come from, where we are, where we're headed. My thoughts drift to my troubled teenage years.

For me, growing up gay in a religious family (as a kid who didn't like to ask questions) was a profound, silent struggle. Being a guy who longed for love with another guy—in conflict with what the 'rule books' said was WRONG—tortured me privately for much of my young life. I knew I was male, but I felt 'less than' other men. There were many dark days. Some darker than I care to share.

My mid-twenties finally brought improvement. Thankfully, I cared enough about my survival to open up and let a little light in on my carefully guarded secret. I gradually discovered acceptance, from my friends, my siblings, my parents—and, most of all, from myself.

Now, at fifty-one, I take a sip of my vodka martini and let myself appreciate my husband, our dog, the warm fire, the life we've built. We can pay our bills, take an occasional vacation, and host a great party.

Still, something about hitting my fifties has thrown up a red flag. Without prompting, a subtle shift has taken place. For the first time, I'm feeling there's more highway in the rearview mirror than in front of the windshield.

I always wanted to sing a top ten hit *(probably not going to happen anytime soon)*.

I always wanted to learn to play the piano like my dad *(my back hurts now when I sit on the piano bench longer than ten minutes)*.

I always wanted to write a bestseller *(it's okay to keep one dream, isn't it?)*.

I sigh, pulling up my hoodie to cover my balding head. My eyes fall on the broken Allison clock on its nearby shelf. The pendulum hangs limp, echoing my mood. I tip my glass and finish its contents. My eyes crawl back to the clock. *When am I gonna start that search for Grandpa Charley's missing collection?*

The Arctic wind rattles the windows, as if it wants to grab me by the shoulders and shake.

Getting up from the couch, I pull the clock from beneath its dome and set it on the coffee table. Next I head to my office, where I dig through my files looking for artifacts. My childhood journals. The fuzzy copy of a California newspaper article my Uncle Gordon mailed to me. A blurry photo of my grandfather's shop on Ventura Blvd. The shop's guest book.

Back on the couch, I'm now surrounded by the past. I reread the article, "Unique Clocks Are Created By Local Jeweler." The reporter had visited my grandfather's store and shared a detailed description of the Allison Mystery Clock. I stare at the photo of the shop for clues. The store's name. The address. Reflections in the front windows. Nothing jumps out.

Maybe an Internet search will turn up something. I retrieve my laptop and begin. "Charles Allison" and "watchmaker" bring up nothing. *The clocks were supposed to go to a museum.* I expand my search. The National Association of Watch & Clock Collectors (NAWCC) museum in Pennsylvania seems like the biggest player. There are many museums in Southern California, some clock-centric, some not.

Right then and there, I start an email campaign: to the NAWCC—have they heard of my grandfather? To random museums in the San Fernando Valley—are the Allison clocks in their collection? To the L.A. Public Library—do they keep records on local artisans? Without much pre-planning, my quest has begun.

'I cannot begin to theorize on the method of operating the clocks I have seen today.'
—Fred Smith, architectural engineer

CHAPTER 3

January 2018

It turns out that looking for your grandfather's missing clock collection in the Information Age is not as easy as you would think. Internet searches turn up a Charles B. Allison who owned a grocery store in Mendicino in 1911. Not my grandpa. He was in Rochester in 1911.

Instead of research, I spend a few hours working on a submission for my monthly writing group. I lay out the story of my dad telling me about Charley's clocks—envisioning that this will eventually turn into a full-blown memoir about a quest to find the Allison collection.

I put my laptop aside and decide to start on some "old school" research. The Allison Watchmakers guest book contains a year-over-year chronicle of my grandfather's shop. I can read that and learn about my grandfather through his customers.

I carefully begin turning through the initial pages, for the first time trying to decipher some of the handwritten entries, not just scanning for familiar names. The book starts on March 9, 1941. I look it up. It was a Sunday.

I feel a connection to my deceased grandfather across the ages. When I started my first journal at ten, I wrote out the date in full on the first entry. No abbreviations of the four-digit year to confuse future generations. *Just like Charley.*

Blanche V. Stuart was the first person to sign. I wonder if she was a friend, getting the initial honor. Or maybe just someone who happened in, someone whose watch was running too slowly. A guy I assume was her husband signed just below her slanted signature.

'Now I have seen everything.'

—Paul Stuart

He must mean the Mystery Clock. I'm glad he commented; entries with a comment are more interesting. I flip forward. Most of them are names I've never heard of.

'Mr. Allison; It is the world's misfortune that they can't all be familiar with your work.'
—*Michael Lawley*

'A true craftsman in a needy world.'
—*G. W. Neubauer*

'He makes "amazing" time. (If you know what I mean).'
—*Norm Woolley*

I keep turning the pages. A few names jump out at me. Bud Abbott! Dana Andrews! Charlie Ruggles! These are celebrities I recognize from some of my favorite black-and-white movies. Some leave comments, some just signatures.

It creeps up on me, but I finally see it. Each signature, each comment tells its own little story. My grandfather's work touched many lives. More than just Hollywood celebrities. Soldiers on leave from the war. A couple out for a Sunday drive.

This book is a treasure. I grab my phone and start methodically snapping a photo of each page, even as I mentally kick myself.

Why have I not digitized this before? What if we'd had a fire or a flood? This one-copy-only book of my grandfather's might not have survived.

I slowly let my stomach relax, as the number of photos on my phone grows. *I'm doing it now.*

That's the most important thing. I may have waited until my fifties to get started, but I'm doing it now.

'I'd like to be able to keep time as well as your clocks and watches do!'
—Gene Krupa, drummer for The Benny Goodman Orchestra

CHAPTER 4

May 2018

In a meandering phone conversation with my sister, Molly, I fill her in on the details of my renewed quest. As the oldest daughter, she had an overlarge share in raising me. She used to tuck me in as a kid and read to me from our family collection of Hardy Boy books.

Molly listens attentively as I read random entries from the shop book.

When I share 'Directed by the hand of God' (from Mrs. Thomas Russell), my sister laughs. "I bet Charley got a load of that," she says.

"Why?"

She tells me she's pretty sure Grandpa Charley was an agnostic who wouldn't allow religion in the house. When Molly was four, she had to live with our Grandma Martha (Charley's second wife) for a whole year, due to a family illness. She soaked in a lot of Gram's stories—and is the go-to source for Allison history. Most of everything she's told me has panned out in my research to date.

"Uncle Gordon 'got saved' right after they moved to California," she says. "That didn't sit well with Charley." She chuckles. "Of course, you've heard the story about how Gordon called for a visit and Charley said, 'You can come over but leave your goddamn Bible at home!'"

Uncle Gordon was Charley's first son, my dad's half-brother. His mom died when he was four. He must have had his own struggles.

I laugh. "Yeah, I've heard that one."

Her tone gets serious. "I do think Old Charley got a bit of religion at the end. Dad told me Charley once carved The Lord's Prayer on the head of a pin."

I take this in. At this point in our lives, I know this story is more important to her, the staunch Catholic, than it is to me. At fifty-two, I fall somewhere on the midpoint of the faith spectrum. As a teenager, I considered becoming a priest. But life's unfolding path has left me with more questions than answers. Questions seem to drive me these days.

A thought pops up. *I need to go to California. That's where answers about Charley are.*

I wrap things up with my sister and start dialing John, a high school friend who relocated to the San Fernando Valley. I give him the quick version of Charley's story and talk about my quest. He offers to put me up for a week in July.

I'm on your trail, Grandpa. Next stop, L.A.

C

CHARLEY'S STORY

(1892 – 1918)

1892

Frank Allison and Alta Beale were married in the late 1800s and, over the next twenty years, had a total of ten children. The third-born, Charles Beale Allison in 1892, was to have a significant career not foretold by his humble roots.

For a reason that is lost to time, half of Frank and Alta's children were born in the Western United States and half were born in Western New York—but not in straight, chronological order. The Allisons led a ping-pong existence between Colorado, Nebraska, and New York for several years.

Frank was a farmer by trade, so perhaps he and Alta went where the growing was good. When the dust finally settled, they made their permanent home in Murray, NY, just thirty miles outside of Rochester. Growing up, Charley would have had one foot in the East and one foot in the West.

Frank (center, back) and Alta (seated, right) Allison gather the family for an unlabeled photo around the turn of the century. My grandfather, Charley, is possibly the boy in the front row.

1908

According to family lore, Charley was sixteen when a local businessman, friendly to the Allisons, noticed the boy's interest in his timepiece: an oversized Gubelin pocket watch.

The man loaned the watch to young Charley so that he could explore its works—carefully—while the man was out of town on business. Possibly it was running slow. Perhaps Charley said "I can fix that for you."

With precision, Charley painstakingly disassembled the entire watch, figuring out the function of its various parts as he went. He cleaned and reassembled it. Despite this 'amateur disruption', the watch ran well afterwards.

When the businessman returned, he was so impressed with Charley's efforts, he gave the watch to the boy. And a watchmaker was born.

This Gubelin pocket watch, recovered in 2022 with the missing collection, gives credence to family lore about the launch of my grandfather's career. At an early age, Charley began branding his work with his last name.

1910

Between siblings, in-laws, and cousins, the Allison clan could always corral a large showing for photos. Being just a buggy ride from downtown Rochester, where George Eastman had recently designed and patented the first Kodak camera, surely helped them have access to inexpensive photography.

The Allisons appear to have been endlessly social. Having so many relations in the area must have lent itself to frequent gatherings. Their multiple group photos tell the tale that family was important.

The extended Allison family show in this undated photo, most likely around 1910. Charley is the young man with the big smile on the left.

1912

Maybe the fact that the Allison siblings had lost three sisters* by the time Charley was fifteen drew the survivors closer together. In photos, they're often teasing or goofing with each other. They couldn't know that more death lay in the near future.

Around 1912, Charley met a young woman named Jean Collins, who'd migrated with her parents from Ontario, Canada to Rochester, New York just three years earlier. They fell in love and married in June 1913, when he was twenty-one and she was twenty.

According to family lore, Charley looked forward to being a father. Son Gordon was born in November 1914. Charley supported his new wife and child by repairing watches. He was especially adept at fine tuning the works for accurate timekeeping. Word of mouth gave him steady business.

Despite cause to celebrate the expansion of the Allison family, that was a difficult decade for Charley and his siblings. They lost a brother, Ralph, at sixteen in 1914, and another brother, Bryan, at twenty-three in 1918.**

Compounding those devastating losses, also in 1918, at the age of twenty-five, Jean pricked her finger on a sewing needle. The wound became infected and she died four days later.

Charley must have been nearly inconsolable.

Jean Collins Allison was my grandfather's first wife. She gave birth to my Uncle Gordon in 1914.

*Cause of death is not included in any family records, but all were under the age of seven.
**Again, no cause of death turned up during author's research.

G

GREG'S STORY

(2018)

'To Mr. Allison, whose clocks are not for an age but for all time.'
—Jean Fountaine, shop visitor

CHAPTER 5

July 2018

It's 100 degrees when I step off the plane. John (eventually) picks me up and mentions that it's 115 degrees back in the Valley. He also explains that he was delayed by giving a spare pair of sneakers to a homeless man, which he'd packed into his car earlier that day.

"How'd you know if you'd see a homeless person?" I ask.

He laughs at my naiveté.

Over beers, we plan my strategy for the coming week. I'll need to get around. An unlimited bus and subway card seems like the best option.

In the past three months, I've been in touch with the local historical society and the L.A. Public Library. One librarian (who I'll call Cathy) gave me some research suggestions. She'd proposed that, from my home in Rochester, I contact a watchmakers institute in Ohio, consult an antiques and collectibles directory at my local library, and research the *Los Angeles Times* online. No luck on all fronts.

If I'm ever in L.A., she'd also suggested some museums to visit and some books in her own library to explore. I've assembled a local 'hit list.'

Before going to bed, I reread the fuzzy articles my Uncle Gordon sent me— just a few years before his death at 93. Not for the last time, I mentally kick myself for not getting more details from the principal players in this tale while they were alive.

Unnamed and undated, they are sketchy artifacts at best. That said, the write-up and embedded photos confirm that a) Allison Watchmakers was at the corner of Ventura and Sepulveda, b) the Allison Mystery Clock existed and was as mysterious as my tipsy father had described, and c) the Allison Clock Collection was destined for an unnamed museum upon my grandfather's death.

At the breakfast table, I plan my day. I'm going to start by visiting the shop's location.

The bus is air conditioned, a sharp contrast to the dry heat everywhere else. I settle into my seat, feeling clammy as the sweat rolling down the inside of my t-shirt chills.

I quickly note that there are homeless people *everywhere*. Pushing carts on the walk to the bus stop. Hanging out in the alley behind the Salvation Army depot. Sleeping in the bus seat a few rows back.

I've seen a few homeless people in Rochester in my life, but nothing approaching this scale. I feel a weird combination of sadness *(how hard it must be!)*, guilt *(why am I not helping more?)*, and apathy *(what can I actually do?)*. I now understand why John laughed at my naiveté upon my arrival.

Traveling south on Sepulveda, I stand at the front of the bus and let my mind wander. Did Charley Allison ride this same bus line? Did he eat at diners on one of these side streets? Did he stop for a drink at a local pub?

My research (and my map app's on-site view) have already confirmed that a high rise office building has replaced the row of stores where my grandfather's shop once stood. We pull up to the corner of Ventura and I disembark. My skin is tingling.

I've come today to get a flavor of the neighborhood, to walk the streets he walked. Pound the pavement, like a TV detective. Yet, the "Mamma Mia Here We Go Again!" poster at the bus stop delivers a sharp reality slap. Seventy years ago is an *awfully* long time. Things change. Finding these clocks might be next-to-impossible.

I cross the street. I have the address memorized. *15310 Ventura Boulevard.* I walk to the spot where Allison Watchmakers would have been.

There is nothing familiar from the newspaper photo with what I'm seeing on the street. No last-minute, movie-plot twist, where an ornate fire hydrant or antique streetlamp gives me assurance. I spot a manhole cover in the sidewalk near the curb. *City of Los Angeles* is carved into its metal bulk.

Maybe that was here back then. Maybe.

For now, it's a start. I close my eyes and listen to the sounds of the Sunday morning traffic.

Grandpa...I'm here.

'To a genius from a watchmaker.'

—Joseph Buckurald, watchmaker

CHAPTER 6

July 2018

Finished with my initial reverie at the corner of Sepulveda and Ventura, I walk toward the bus stop and encounter another homeless person. He's sleeping on a brick planter. He's wearing relatively clean jeans and a concert t-shirt. One sock is on, one sock is off; a white plastic grocery bag is clutched in his left hand.

I've started to realize that the homeless are a part of everyday life in L.A.—but I wasn't prepared for him to be attractive! About my age, with short-cropped, white hair and olive skin. I wonder if he's homeless or just a party animal? I consider taking his photo, then cringe away in shame.

I'm back on the bus.

The rest of the day is less scripted. It's Sunday, so most research places are closed. To pass the time, I look at a bus-brochure map of L.A. It's like a shout out from TV shows and movies I grew up with. The towns: Beverly Hills. Malibu. Santa Barbara. The boulevards: Ventura. Sunset.

I decide to scope out the ride to the downtown library, so I'll know where to go on Monday. I pull up my map app, looking at nearby sites. One little flag catches my attention, just off Ventura Boulevard. *The Brady Bunch house.*

With a Sunday afternoon to kill in L.A., to a Gen Xer like me, it's enough of a draw that I decide to take a twenty-minute detour and check it out. I take a selfie and post it to Facebook. It quickly racks up a lot of comments.

My afternoon is devoted to downtown. After a quick lunch and a beer *(what the hell, I'm on vacation)*, I ride one more bus to a subway and, an hour later, I'm walking the streets of L.A.

It's much hillier than I had imagined. The roads slope and stretch in all directions and altitudes. My stroll to the library becomes a hike.

For all of my research, it did not occur to me that the library would be open on Sunday. But here it is, doors wide all afternoon, in air-conditioned glory. I enter. *Will I find Grandpa Charley's obituary—maybe even the clocks—on my first time out?*

A few things strike me right away: the coldness of the A/C (in my sweat-drenched t-shirt, I'm already feeling clammy); the grand architecture with arched, painted ceilings (like the churches I've visited in France and Italy); the number of homeless people (I continue to struggle somewhere between compassion, judgment, and avoidance).

The Information Desk is my first stop. They give me two choices: Up to the second floor, for the Arts and Music department, which might have information on clocks, or down to Basement Level -4, for the History department, which has old newspapers and records.

I head up.

On the second floor, I approach the desk and speak to my first librarian of the day. She is thin, tall, with a dominant splash of gray in her hair and a trademark set of reading glasses dangling from her neck.

At this point, having repeated my story to historians, museum curators, and friends, I've got my talk track down—The Mystery of the Missing Grandfather's Clocks (ha ha). I launch my pitch.

"Hi. I'll give you the short version of a long story—but, basically, I'm looking for the obituary of my grandfather who died in 1955 in Sherman Oaks. He was a watchmaker and I'm trying to figure out what happened to his missing clock collection." I take a breath.

Her brow furrows. She stares at me; the squint of her eyes reveals a window to precision and thoughtfulness.

"This is sounding very familiar," she says.

I pull out a hard copy of my email correspondence from three months ago. "Are you Cathy by any chance?"

She nods in the affirmative. *What were the chances I'd meet her on my first try? I'm putting this in the 'good omen' category.*

Cathy scans the email printout. "Yes, now I remember. Your grandfather was from somewhere in New York, I believe. Did you follow any of my suggestions?"

I nod. I'm alternately excited to have connected live with her—and also disappointed that her leads were dead ends.

"I did. Nothing really turned up any information. But I was hoping being here in person would help." I pull out my thick folder of notes. "I'm ready to put in the legwork. The Information Desk suggested a visit to the basement archives to look through the local newspapers."

I show her the fuzzy article copies—and I pull out photos of a couple of celebrity signatures from the shop book, hoping to reel her in. *Dana Andrews. Mary Astor. Bud Abbott.*

In my fantasy movie version of this moment, the montage rolls (possibly to the tune of *St. Elmo's Fire*) as she's fascinated by my quest. We roll up our sleeves and spend the next three days slurping coffee in the archives. We wrap with a 'thumbs up' picture for the *L.A. Times* under the headline "Librarian Licks Lost Legacy—Grandson and Grandclocks Reunited."

The reality is *way less fun.*

"The guest book is a good artifact," she says, scanning my pictures. "Given that his shop was in Sherman Oaks, these newspaper articles might be articles from *The Van Nuys News*." She pulls out a sticky note and scribbles a couple of reference numbers. "You can look through our art collection reference on this floor. Some of them cover clockmaking." She hands me the note. "But your best chances are probably in the local archives, down in the basement, Level Four.

"Thank you," I say, packing my research materials back into my bookbag. "I guess time will tell!"

She smiles. "Good luck," she says, then turns to help somebody else.

Moving to the art history section, I consult the reference numbers on the post-it note and pull a few thick volumes off the designated shelf. With my bookbag in tow, I retreat to a wooden table by myself.

After 30 minutes of trolling articles about the history of clockmaking from Moscow to Minneapolis, I give up. These are books about fancy clocks from museums around the world. There's nothing local about my grandfather. *Cathy was right. My best bet is the archives.*

Exchanging farewell waves with the librarian, I head to SubBasement 4. When the doors open, I sneeze. *Musty.*

I locate the Information Desk. A slightly younger, hippie version of Cathy (short brown hair, khaki pants and a long-sleeved t-shirt) is on the phone. I wait.

When she's free, I repeat my spiel. She actually seems impressed with the celebrity names I throw out. *Fibber McGee. Molly. Charlie Ruggles.* She reviews the copies of the two newsprint articles. I explain that, unfortunately, the source newspaper is not named.

"We have several local newspapers on microfilm." She points to the fuzzy articles. "These are most likely from *The Van Nuys News and Valley Green Sheet.*"

I've heard of the former, but not the latter. "Are those two different publications?"

She smiles. "No—they just changed their name at one point. They were *The Van Nuys News* some of the time and *The Van Nuys News and Valley Green Sheet* later. What month and year would you like to start with?"

I think for a moment. "How about February 1955? If I can find his obituary, it might tell me what happened to his estate."

On her computer, she orders up reels for February and March 1955. A short time later, a young man places a couple of small cardboard boxes on the counter.

She nods to me and scoops up the boxes. "Here's your spools. If you bring them down to the microfilm readers, the people at that desk can help you get started." I walk in the direction she points and, within ten minutes, I'm seated at a microfilm viewing machine and ready to go.

I use the automatic scroll button to scan quickly through most of the reel, the motion of which threatens to sour my stomach. I suck on a mint and keep going. I land on the late February issue and turn through the pages more slowly.

Skimming, I locate the obituaries under 'Vital Statistics' and read through the entries. Ellen Ann Evans. Carl L. Moen. *No Charles B. Allison.* Under 'Births', I note forty-plus birth listings for that week. *The baby boomers.*

I load up the March roll and continue my painstaking search. Turning pages more slowly reduces my queasy feeling. No listing of my grandfather's death jumps out.

I've now been on Floor -4 for over an hour. I am seized by a sneezing fit; my throat is scratchy; I feel a little like I need to lay down.

Fortunately, being a perennial allergy sufferer, I've come prepared. I pop an antihistamine and wash it down with a sip from my water bottle. I know this will make me sleepy, so I decide to wrap for the day. I can do a more careful review with better preparation. *Mental note: bring caffeine tomorrow!*

Outside the library, the downtown buildings cast long shadows, but the oppressive heat remains—especially outside of the frigid sub-basement. Again, I'm surprised that everything in downtown L.A. seems on a slope. *It looks flatter on TV!*

I catch an afternoon subway and time the ride, including a transfer to bus, then a short walk. *94 minutes. Need to build travel time into my week's schedule.*

My first day has been a bit of a bust. But one of my mom's favorite movie quotes floats across my mind—it feels more powerful here in the shadow of Hollywood. *Tomorrow is another day.*

'I've seen some of the finest specimens of watchmaker's art in many European countries but I must say that Allison has them all beat.'

—R. B. *Stone, DDS*

CHAPTER 7

July 2018

It's Monday. I have a couple of research days left but, if yesterday taught me anything, this doesn't look to be a quick payoff.

The sidewalk seems hot enough to fry the proverbial egg, even at 8 a.m. Unlike most people I know—including my husband, my friends, my writing students—this is not a problem for me. I love the heat.

On the bus, the A/C is so severe, I again feel chilly with my sweaty scalp and armpits. *How do people dress up for work here?* I wonder what my grandfather, a Rochester native, wore in 1940s L.A., pre-air-conditioning. *Did he dress up and sweat? Was he always cold, like me, and enjoyed the steamy California days?*

I retrace my trip from yesterday. *Did Charley ever ride the underground trains?* I can only guess. Being from Rochester, I envision him as more car native. But, being an inventor, he'd be intrigued by the engineering feats involved with the tunnels. I settle on a definite *maybe*.

Emerging from the subway, I grab a cup of tea from Starbucks and head for SubBasement 4. There is a different librarian—a skinny guy with gray hair and a graying beard. I decide to forego my spiel and simply request newspaper reels from 1955 (the year Charley died) and 1941 (the year of the first entries in the shop book).

The microfilm arrives and I set up shop in the same cube as the day before. I take a preemptive allergy pill.

If no obit surfaces, maybe I can find the source of one of Uncle Gordon's newspaper articles. Or maybe an announcement of the store's opening. It's a shot. *There are movie star signatures in the guest book, for God's sake! Somebody must have chronicled him!*

I turn through page after page of the microfilm, much more slowly than yesterday. My thorough search takes more time. One hour, then another passes.

Headlines continue to catch my attention. I ignore some articles, but others— I can't resist.

Pedestrian Walked Right Through Car
Screen Star in Hospital After Plane Crash
Third Atom Test Flash Seen Over Five States

My stomach rumbles and I'm a little bored with no solid results. Why is there no obituary of my grandfather in this local paper? Isn't that standard procedure, even in 1955?

A text from my sister, Judy, is a welcome break. As the two youngest Allison children, she and I developed a strong bond early in life.

How's the trip going?

My five siblings are interested in my journey's outcome. We've all heard the clocks stories since we were kids. I tap out a response.

Striking out on any Charley info. I am looking thru microfilm of old newspapers trying to find his obit. So far…nada.

Her reply comes back quickly.

Im sure you know but supposedly his new wife's son got the clocks.

I stare at the tiny screen. In spite of the antihistamine malaise, I can feel my blood pressure rise. My heart speeds up.

I TOTALLY did not know that! Where'd you hear that? The newspaper article from Uncle Gordon says they were supposed to go to a museum.

I feel like saying something significantly more snarky—why am I just hearing this now? I've been researching for months and I've kept my family up-to-date. But my sister Judy is a good person; rereading her text, I recognize she thought I knew. The pounding in my chest ratchets down a notch as I wait for her reply.

I think i heard that from uncle gordon

Thanks that is a big help. I've been focused on museums. I've been kicking myself for not asking Gordon more about it when he was alive. Do you have any more details?

Something at work must have distracted her; it's a couple of minutes before her response. I fidget in my cubicle chair and look through my notes.

My phone dings.

Sorry, don't really have any more details other than his name might have been tommy. Maybe you can find the wife's name.

27

Yeah, I think I will focus my search on her now. thanks.

I feel a little like crying as I unwind the microfilm. This changes everything. If some distant relative has the clocks in their attic, I'll probably never find them.

Another one of my pre-trip, fantasy montages surfaces, rubbing salt in the wound. In this one, I hit the L.A. archives, find an obituary, visit a dozen museums, and finally stumble across a friendly, elderly woman with half-glasses, who leads me into their "American Inventors" wing and presents my grandfather's clocks. She even has a tear in her eye, having found the long-lost heir to these priceless relics.

In real life, it's like sifting piles of sand on the beach to find the car key you dropped seventy years ago. *Maybe it's good that I chose writing over research as a career. I don't seem to be that good of a detective after all.*

I pack up my book bag and head for fresher air.

'The interest to me in these clocks is their beauty of material
and delightful individuality and usefulness.'

—Edith Heim, shop visitor

CHAPTER 8

July 2018

The next morning, I'm back in SubBasement 4, on the other side, where the ancestry computers are. If I'm going to find these clocks, I need to focus on my grandfather's third wife.

I start small, plugging in my grandfather's name and looking for marriage licenses. 10,082 records. *Yeesh.*

I start adding variables to the search as I know them. Charles B Allison. Born 1892. Died 1955. Lived in Rochester, NY and Sherman Oakes, CA. I plug in the shop address, where I know he lived.

A name pops up in the 1940 census image. The address is a match. I expand and read the line next to my grandfather's. Grace Allison—listed as wife at the same address! Now I have a name.

I start a search for records of Charles Allison and Grace Allison. Again, there are more than 10,000 records. The wealth and woes of search engines. I pull out my bag of trail mix and start clicking though the more promising artifacts.

The 1939 phone directory lists Charley and Grace, at the watch shop. Another screen displays a record from Mexico. It's in Spanish. I almost skip it, but the English translation shows both Charley's and Grace's names. I click on the image.

A marriage license pops up from April 18, 1933. I can make out the name of the city (Juarez, Chihuahua) but I don't read Spanish and, even with three years of high school Latin, the rest is pretty indecipherable. Except—the names of the bride and groom, in the thin, swirly script of some long-dead Mexican office clerk, leap out at me. *Grace Reynolds* and *Charles Allison.*

They went to Mexico to get married? Why a marriage south of the border?

I now have his third wife's first and last name. The computer's internal fan revs up as my search intensifies. There are several Grace Reynolds in our country's history. I click through them, trying to pick those who were born around the same time as my grandfather.

Grace Reynolds, born 1890. I dig into her a little bit.

I note that she shows up married, in 1916, to a guy named Paul. Maybe this is not my Grace. Except—I click on their marriage certificate and note the location: *Rochester N.Y.!*

I know my grandfather cheated on Grandma Martha around 1930; that's the reason they separated. It never occurred to me that the 'other woman' would also be married. But now I have Grace and Charles in the same city, during the same years. I keep digging.

By the 1930 census, Grace and Peter have two daughters and live in Rochester, NY. No son (maybe named 'Tommy'—the one who Uncle Gordon said might have ended up with the clocks). Maybe my grandfather had another child with this woman? I've never heard anything like that.

By the 1940 census, Grace and Charley are living alone in the back of the watch store in Sherman Oaks, CA.

What happened during those ten years? In my mind's eye, I imagine these two couples, Charley and Gram, with two boys (my father and Uncle Gordon) and Peter and Grace, with two girls. All of them living in Rochester; all struggling through the Great Depression. With an extra-marital affair linking them. What a mess it must have been.

I take a break and text my progress to my oldest sister, Molly. She's intrigued by the Mexican wedding and texts me back.

I wonder if they got married in Mexico
because Charley never divorced Gram?

It's an interesting theory, but the day is wearing on and my throat is scratchy, even with the allergy pill. I think about wrapping up. One more text from Molly comes in.

I remember Dad telling me that the last time
he visited Charley at the shop on the way
home from the war (circa 1945),
Charley introduced him to Marge.

This is another story I do not recall ever hearing! What is up with the wealth of sister stories coming at me now that I am actually in L.A.?

I give Molly a call and sort through the details. Could he possibly have said Grace, not Marge? Molly doesn't think so. And she has a good memory for family details. Now I'm stuck. Did Grandpa marry a fourth woman named Marge, after Grace? If that's true, then *her* son could be the elusive 'Tommy.'

The 1950 census should tell me who was living at the shop. I eat a handful of nuts to recharge and click back on Ancestry.com. No 1950 census records come up. I do a quick Internet search for details on 'census records release.'

To protect the privacy of the living, U.S. census records are publicly released only after seventy years have elapsed.

I do the math. I won't be able to see the 1950 census for another two years.

I hang my head and stare at my bag of trail mix for several moments. I can hear the khaki-sporting librarian talking to someone at the desk. A fruit fly circles my snacks. I don't bother to swat it away.

Squelching a couple of sneezes into my hoodie, I log off the computer and pack my book bag.

I'm not going to solve any mysteries this trip.

C

CHARLEY'S STORY

(1919 – 1932)

1919

Despite the devastating loss of his wife, with a young son and a thriving business to care for, Charley was most likely in a rush to remarry.

He met Martha Gratton Hite in 1918. Although she was only 26, she also knew the loss of a spouse—she'd married her high school sweetheart in 1911, only to lose him overseas to World War I. The common bond of loss likely drew Charley and Mart to each other. Within a year of Jean's death, Mart became Mrs. Martha Allison.

Mart (my grandmother) and Charley were likely drawn to each other through mutual loss.

1920

Mart welcomed Charley's son Gordon as her own—but insisted on a suitable home. Charley, doing very well in the watch business, promised to build her a brick house in East Rochester, if she would bear him a second child. She agreed.

Although Charley longed to have a daughter, fate planned otherwise. In August 1920, Darwin was born. He was christened with the middle name of 'Bryan', becoming the namesake of Charley's recently deceased little brother.

That same day, Charley broke ground for their new home. According to census records, he was no stranger to housebuilding. Sometime during his teenage years, his own father, Frank, had transitioned from farming to construction. In addition to watchmaking, Charley must have had years of construction experience under his belt.

Family lore tells that he spent $20,000 on the East Rochester project, equivalent to $300K in 2023. Charley himself directed (and participated in) the entire effort.

The blended family soon had one of the finest homes in the area, a smart brick structure with matching garage, right on Main Street.

Gordon, Martha, and Darwin (my dad) at their newly built East Rochester home, 1925.

1932

For over a decade, the East Rochester Allisons were a happy family—at least on the surface.

In 1932, Gordon graduated as valedictorian of his high school class. Twelve-year-old Darwin showed a natural aptitude for the piano and taught himself to play by ear. Mart and Charley enjoyed a circle of friends among the local business class.

They stayed in close touch with extended family—both in the Rochester area and across the country in Los Angeles (where Mart and Charley each had relatives). Cheery postcards and photos flowed back and forth through the U.S. Postal System.

But the surface never tells the full story.

Charley and Martha, pictured with my father, Darwin, had a happy marriage—at least on the surface, 1926.

G

GREG'S STORY

(2019)

CHAPTER 9

February 2019

Our third-floor windows have a thin layer of frost covering the outside. It's after dinner and I'm fidgety. My husband has settled in front of the TV with a Moscow mule. I want one…but I've made a new year's resolution to add more alcohol-free days to my life—so, today, I'm abstaining.

Alcohol has crept up on me. I recall my father's own troubled relationship with it. He was in his sixties when I was a teen. It wasn't every night that Drinking Dad emerged—but at least two or three times a week.

I've also learned in the years after his death to cut my dad some slack.

My research has given me insight into the difficulties he endured. I've come to respect my dad's life-hurdles: growing through his teens with a dad who lived on the opposite coast. Going to war halfway around the world in his early twenties, an age when one of my big concerns was managing too much credit card debt. Being unemployed at fifty during the troubled economy of the 1970s. *No wonder he drank.*

In my mid-twenties, I made my way through 'children of alcoholics' literature and counseling. I know that kids like me are more prone to repeat the sins of our fathers—so I stay cautious.

In my thirties, my husband and I enjoyed an occasional beer. We poked private fun at our retired neighbors, who sipped martinis on their porch every evening.

Somewhere along the road to middle age, the hard stuff crept in. We hosted big-screen TV events for our friends—and my husband discovered a propensity for mixology. We bought our first liquor cabinet by the time I turned forty.

Now, in our fifties, we have *become* the couple next door. We have a wide variety of beverages to choose from and, most nights, we have a cocktail with dinner—and maybe a second (or third) with post-dinner TV.

Which brings me to my new year's resolution. There are some legacies from my father I'd like to avoid—diabetes and excessive drinking top the list. Like sugar, alcohol is now on my list of things to limit.

With nothing better to do on this wintry night, I wander into my third-floor office. I like this room; it's one of the few places in the house that is exclusively my space. I feel less inclined to keep it tidy. I wrote most of my first book here, holed up in a glorified closet with a slanted ceiling and no windows.

I snap on the lights and fire up my ancient desktop computer. With these all running, the office becomes toasty enough that I can relax—even on a depressingly chilly February evening. I sink into the comfort.

I pop open my fire safe. In my imagination, other adults keep things like house deeds, cash, and stocks in a fire safe. Me? Allison Watchmakers guest book. My high-school theology notebook. My collection of personal journals, which I started at ten.

I pull out one journal at random, from 1989, when I was twenty-three. It starts with a winter trip my mom and I were prepping for—a drive from New York to California. Just the two of us, delivering a car to my sister, then flying home.

In the entry, we'd planned a February night of fun at my apartment (twenty minutes from my parents' house) before an early morning departure. Dad called to check on us—he'd been watching the national news tracking an ice storm across the country.

I turn through the pages, fondly remembering the few days of pre-trip weather delays, during which my mom and I stayed at my apartment, renting movies and ordering pizzas. Since my mom was with me while dad was home alone, we called my father every day—much more than I normally did.

I flip the page and freeze. Here is the record of a 1989 conversation I have thoroughly forgotten.

Clues to the Allison Clocks
Marjorie Smith – Charley Allison, married 1940 or 41
Son from previous marriage: Jimmy Smith
She lives in the back of the clock shop
She is 86 in 1989

How could I have forgotten this?!

Molly was right. There was another wife after Grace, named Marge. And there's Judy's report from Uncle Gordon that his wife's son, possibly named Tommy, ended up with the clocks. *Tommy sounds an awful lot like Jimmy.*

I now have a clear target for my quest.

Well...clear as mud. Could there be a more generic name than Jimmy Smith? I have my work cut out for me.

'There's more than seven wonders.'

–Dan Arthur, shop visitor

CHAPTER 10

March 2019

I am driving from Rochester to Richmond for a work meeting. I receive a phone call from an unfamiliar number with a Buffalo area code. I don't answer. If it's important, they'll leave a message.

The voicemail icon pops up a couple of minutes later. I listen. It's Ed from the local Chapter 13 of the National Watch & Clock Collectors association. He received a report of my new membership to the national organization and wants to invite me to join the local meetings.

I save the message, resolving to call him back when I have some time. *Some free time.*

A few months later I am driving to D.C. in my new-to-me RAV4. My first car where my cell phone talks directly to the vehicle. Work has been busy for months—I've been terribly negligent with my clock quest. But now I have a few free hours. I call Ed back.

"Hello?" His voice sounds friendly, relaxed at 10 a.m. on a weekday. *Retired?*

"Hi, this is Greg Allison. I'm sorry it's taken me so long to call you back. I joined the national NAWCC and you wanted to tell me about the local Rochester organization."

"Yes, Greg, hello! Let me tell you a little bit about Chapter 13." Through the car's speakers, I can hear his passion for clocks as he describes the meeting dates (monthly, alternating between Rochester and Buffalo), the officers (names I've never heard), the dues ($10 a year). "Your timing is good—we actually have our annual picnic next month. I'd like to invite you as my guest."

"If I'm not traveling for work, that would be great, thank you. I'm also looking for some local clock repair, if you can give me some advice." I give him the full Charley Allison overview, which hits all the points of the clock collection, the movie stars, the left-winding clock as wedding present, the right-turning dad as destroyer. "Because it's so unique, I want to be really careful about who works on it."

Ed is quiet for a moment. "You live in Rochester, right?"

"Yes."

"There aren't a lot of people who do specialty work, but I'll recommend Laurie. If she can't do it herself, she might be able to recommend somebody." He gives me her contact information, which I scratch into a notebook on my lap.

"Thank you, Ed, this is a big help."

"Happy to help, Greg. And I hope to see you at the July picnic."

"Sounds good."

I call Laurie's number immediately. It rolls to voicemail. I leave a short message about needing some specialty clock repair services. Her voice sounds friendly on her recording. I have renewed hope that I will soon have this clock working once again.

The conical, lush hills of Northern Pennsylvania rise in the distance, lifting my thoughts to drift over the slopes. I can almost hear the sound of sweet chimes ringing from the repaired Allison clock, its revival mending seventy years of shame.

Laurie returns my call within a day and we set up an appointment. Back home a few days later, I make the twenty-minute drive from downtown Rochester out to Laurie's workshop.

Her home is set back in a cul-de-sac—as I pull into the drive, a man on a riding lawn mower waves to me from what looks to be an acre of grass. I park near the garage and gingerly transfer the cloth-wrapped Mini-Grandfather from my car's drink tray to my messenger bag.

At the door, I take a deep breath and ring the bell. A woman with brown, shoulder-length hair and a striped t-shirt answers.

"You must be Greg," she says, motioning me inside.

"That's me!" I reply. Her friendly nature reminds me of my sisters as we enter her kitchen.

"Do you do clock repair full time?" I ask her.

She laughs. "Since my husband and I retired from Kodak, it certainly fills up my time."

She gives me a short history of how she got interested in clock repair in 1999 and took courses from local Chapter 13 members. She doesn't tout her credentials, but I know from talking to Ed she's the best in the area. Her easy confidence engenders my trust.

We head down to her basement workshop. She walks me through her collection, which is impressive, to say the least. There's an Ithaca Calendar Clock, built around the turn of the nineteenth century, that is smart enough to know when leap year is. There's a German trumpet clock that has little trumpeters inside. Laurie has the outer case pulled off for repair and she shows me how the gears, figures, and a small bellows interact. So creative and, in contrast to the age of electronics, so very mechanical.

"So why don't you tell me a little bit of what you need," she says. I pull out a copy of the newspaper articles and photos of my grandfather and his shop. I can see by the expression on her face that she's genuinely interested as I fill her in on my search to date.

"And here's the main attraction." I pull the Mini-Grandfather from my shoulder bag and unwrap the cloth.

She takes it carefully into her hands. "Well, I've never seen one like this." Laurie points to a small broken gear in the bottom of the case—something I've never noticed before. The drive here must have shaken it out of the works higher up.

"It probably just needs a new click wheel," she says. "I normally work on bigger clocks; this is more like watch size. But if you can leave it with me, I'll take a look at it."

"Absolutely." We chat for another twenty minutes before I say goodbye. I pull out of her driveway feeling the excitement of success. My grandfather's clock will soon be working again! It's in good hands.

Laurie emails me three days later. She's provided some general observations, but invites me to call for more details. I punch in her number.

"I've given this clock a lot of thought and I honestly think I'm not the right person for the job," she says. My heart sinks a little.

"It's a watch-sized job and I'm more of a clock specialist. I'm not even sure where you could take it. The two watch guys I would have trusted with this have passed away."

I glance out my office window. Sun is glittering off the ripples in my neighbor's pool, but the idyllic summer scene is not delivering any joy.

"Do you have any ideas about what I should do next?"

"Well, you might find someone in the Amish community. They do a lot of watch repair."

"How would I get ahold of them? I imagine they don't have a website."

She chuckles. "No, I imagine not. You could ask Ed. He might know of somebody."

Ed already sent me to Laurie. This isn't going as I'd hoped. "Okay, I'll circle back with him. I'm supposed to see him at the picnic next month. I'll bring the clock to show him."

"I'll be there too."

I sigh. "I'm sorry to sound so disappointed. I was just really hoping to hear those chimes ring again."

"Actually, I think the pendulum and chimes are just for decoration. I don't think they'll do anything."

I wonder if she can hear my heart sink through the phone line.

"Okay. I appreciate your willingness to look at it."

"No problem. It was a pleasure. I'm just sorry I can't help you."

We make arrangements for me to drive out and pick up the clock. As I hang up, the frustration of this quest flushes over me, fresh and raw. *The collection is still missing. There might not be anyone alive who can fix the broken clock. And, even if I do get it fixed, I won't hear the chimes ring.*

I waited too long. There might not be any way to make this dream come true.

The clock might stay broken. The collection might stay missing. *I might not learn more about these men I come from.*

I glance back out the window. A squirrel is in our garden, doing acrobatics on the tomato cages. He jumps effortlessly among the vines without missing a beat.

I have to keep trying. I need to go back to L.A.

CHAPTER 11

July 2019

Is rage hereditary? Pressure builds inside my head, something that wants answers without asking questions. Something that wants to be smart without looking stupid. Something that wants to smash its fist into the gas pump's tiny video display, which is currently offering me a large fountain soda for just 99 cents.

TWELVE HOURS EARLIER: My plane lands in Sacramento. The game plan is a little different this year. My sister Molly owns a used car in Northern California that she wants me to drive back to her in Rochester. To make it all work, I've decided that I'll fly into Sacramento, pick up the car, drive to Los Angeles, do my research, then spend four days driving home. An adventure.

I catch a ride from the airport to the vehicle, a 2011 Ford Focus. It's late, so I check into a nearby hotel. I'll begin my trek early in the morning—I'm thinking of making a day of it and exploring some sights on my journey. Also, my L.A. friend, John, is meeting me halfway, in Bakersfield, to tour the Sequoias.

My sunrise departure does not go as planned. First, I oversleep. And having a car in California, which I thought would be a big asset, has also proven itself a small burden.

It starts with something as simple as gassing up. The tank's nearly empty, so I pull into a Chevron station next to the hotel. I park at a pump, turn it off, get out—only to realize the fuel door is on the passenger side (I've never understood the logic of this automotive design choice). I feel my blood pressure wanting to rise, but it's the first full day of vacation and I have a fantastic quest before me. No worries.

I move to the other side of the island. I swipe my debit card and stick the nozzle into my car. Nadda. Something is wrong with this pump? It happens.

I move to a different island. I swipe my debit card and stick the nozzle into my car. It pumps $1.09 and quits. Now my blood pressure inches up the scale, regardless of my internal reassurances.

I've got it! I never called the bank to say I'd be traveling. I remember once they put a hold on my debit card when I flew to a different state without pre-notice. Usually they text me when this happens…but who am I to split hairs. Still no worries, I have plenty of cash; I'll just prepay inside the station.

I quickly execute that plan—casually mentioning to the clerk that I couldn't get my debit card to work, that I need to fill up and I don't know how much gas this car will take, but that I'll put $40 down and retrieve any change afterwards. She is a short woman with long dark hair and bright eyes. I see empathy reflected in them as she nods at me and takes my money.

I return to Island #2 and pump $4.01—and it quits.

Without prompting, my mind flips back to a memory of my father at his store one Saturday when I was eleven.

He was stacking spaghetti boxes on the shelf. One of them opened a crack and a few rods fell out. He swore ("god-DAMMIT!") while managing to grab the rest before they spilled onto the floor. Tipping the box up, he examined the rupture and told me to get the scotch tape. I retrieved it quickly. As he began to seal the one end, the other end cracked open—and spaghetti tumbled out.

It didn't happen in slow motion, like people sometimes describe scary events. The sweep of his arm was fast as he threw the box across the aisle. It struck a display case and spaghetti exploded in every direction. My father turned and walked to the back storage room. I slunk to the utility closet, grabbed the broom and dustpan, and cleaned up the mess.

Instead of punching the pump display (like I want to), I replace the nozzle and march back inside, resolving to claim my change and go somewhere else for gas. I remind the clerk of my pump number and I watch her eyebrows rise as she counts out $35.99 in change. She grabs a penny from a small cup on the counter and makes it an even $36. I say nothing.

I take the money and turn to leave.

"Did you have trouble?" she asks. In another situation, I would be celebrating her attention to customer service. Today, I just want to find a gas station where I can figure out how the game is played. But I swivel back.

"I couldn't get it to work; I'll just go somewhere else."

"Okay," she says—but her tone rises at the end, making it feel more like a question.

I turn to leave a second time.

"Did you push the nozzle all the way in?" she asks.

Oh! Now I get it! California's emissions protections! I pivot a second time. "You mean it won't pump if you don't push the nozzle far enough into the tank?"

She smiles. "Yes, yes."

"Okay—I'll try it again with my debit card."

The clerk nods as I leave. Armed with this California insider intel, I return to the pump and successfully fill the tank. I have now spent the first half hour of my grand adventure getting gas.

As I pull out of the station, I recall a story about Grandpa Charley.

Back in the 1920s, my grandfather was driving through Macedon, our rural hometown twenty minutes east of Rochester, where most of my grandmother's family lived. Heading back toward the city, he approached a small bridge—one of many in our area that crisscrossed the Erie Canal. I imagine it was a summer evening, because the story reports that his driver's window was down. It was near dusk.

A man walking along the side of the road flagged him down. Charley stopped the car. The man approached. "You can't drive up there. The bridge is closed—they're doing some work on it," he said.

My grandfather reportedly reached out, grabbed the man by the collar, and slammed his face into the edge of the car's roof.

"Don't tell me what to do," he said and drove on.

This story has always sounded crazy to me—but, as I recognize my own resistance to direction from others, I feel a generational connection. I wonder if he made it across the bridge? I wonder why he was so provoked by such a helpful gesture? Was he angry before the man stopped him?

I ease the car onto the California highway ramp, recognizing I'd never do anything as violent as my grandfather. I might do something as violent as my father—the gas pump encounter has brought me close to spaghetti-flinging mode. I wonder if my severe aggravations are a DNA connection up the paternal chain. I also wonder if I'll ever get comfortable asking questions without feeling stupid.

I take a call from John and finalize arrangements for our meetup. The drive from Sacramento to Bakersfield will be a leisurely four hours. I search through my phone for some road trip music. My husband has loaded me up with a few new albums. I pick *Everyone is Here* by the Finn Brothers and turn up the volume.

My husband explained to me that the brothers wrote and recorded the songs after the passing of their mother. Given this context, the first track, *Won't Give In,* has grown on me in the past few weeks.

Listening to it today, the words come alive. The lyrics question what it means to belong to someone. What it means to carry your birth name forward. The singers' conclusion: it means that they won't give in.

Something inside my chest loosens. *I was born with Charley's last name. It's mine to carry on. I belong to it. I can't ever give up on this search.*

When the song ends, I click the repeat button. The warm California sun streams through the car's windows as the song flows over me a second time. On either side of the highway, low hills present occasional tufts of trees surrounded by wheat and grass. My eyes tear at the vastness of it all—the song, my search, the scenery. *I won't give in. I won't give in.*

'To The Finest Watch Maker on this Earth and Creator of Beautiful Clocks.'
—Madam Zetta, shop visitor

CHAPTER 12

July 2019

In Bakersfield, I get a hotel right next to a draft beer pub. John arrives and we celebrate our friendship the usual way—over several pints. The next day, the Sequoias and my first California earthquake (I felt nothing!) capture my attention. We make it to John's house in L.A. by dusk—just in time to light sparklers with his kids in the driveway to celebrate the Fourth.

The next morning, I'm back on mission.

I wake early and notice right away: it's cooler this year. My morning trip to the library is in the 60s, not 80s.

On the way downtown, I stop again at the corner of Ventura and Sepulveda— Allison Watchmaker's former location. What am I really looking for? I want some connection with my grandfather, but how much can I really admire him? Four wives and cheated on my grandmother? Assaulted a guy trying to give him a 'bridge out' warning? Genius watchmaker who invented a mystery clock? It's such a mixed bag.

Yet something has drawn me back to this street corner. *I won't give in. I won't give in.* I stand on the manhole cover and close my eyes, picturing my grandfather, maybe stepping outside of the shop to smoke a cigar, watching the afternoon traffic on Ventura Blvd.

I open my eyes and look around. His view would have been so different in the 1950s. Before the Santa Ana highway. Before the Sherman Oaks Galleria. Is there anything I can touch across the seventy years that separate us?

I walk up to the corner and look right. A line of hills to the south down Sepulveda would have been here. It's not much. But it's something.

I'm back in SubBasement 4's ancestry section. I settle at the same computer as on my last visit. I'm within ear-and-eye distance of the information desk. The same hippie librarian is here, with her horn-rimmed reading glasses, now-collar-length brown hair, and her no-nonsense attitude about helping people with their research.

She's talking with a peer about watching a neighbor's dog. I can't help but overhear:

"I brought him to my house but he barked his head off at 1:30 a.m. so I took him back home today and put him in his crate." She pauses and frowns. "I'm a cat person. I know it's supposedly comforting for dogs to lounge in their crate space, but something about putting an animal in a cage doesn't sit right with me."

I chuckle to myself, thinking this is a quintessential California hippie conversation. I set out my trail mix, down an allergy pill, and begin.

I'm armed with two more names this year: Marjorie and James Smith.

Records under these names abound. Over the next hour, I run down a number of rat holes, not finding anything that links to Charley or Allison Watchmakers. Maybe he never married Margie?

The librarians are now talking about yesterday's quake. Apparently the SubBasement 4 overhead light fixtures had swayed.

Even with the antihistamine, my throat starts to feel scratchy and my nose hair begins to tickle. I start to feel sick, like I need to lay down in fresh air. I hate to leave without advancing the search.

I decide to focus on Jimmy—the one person in my research who might still be alive. If he and Margie still lived at Allison Watchmakers after Charley's death in 1955, that would be my first clue to where the clocks might have ended up.

From prior research, I've learned that phone books are on microfilm. I need the hippie librarian to direct me to the reels. She's helpful again, walking me past several aisles to a row of blue-gray file cabinets. Consulting the drawer labels, she pulls one open. Small brown boxes fill the space.

"San Fernando, 1956, San Fernando, 1956," she chants, picking through the boxes. "Wow," she says, staring into the drawer. "It looks like the archives jump from 1951 to 1962." She looks up at me. "I'm sorry, I don't know why."

"Maybe they're misfiled," I suggest.

We look through the rest of the drawer—no luck.

Why is the Universe working suddenly working against me? I pull out 1951 and 1962, and start with the earlier one. Maybe Margie and Jimmy will be listed with Charley; that might give me a middle initial, at least.

I scroll to the correct page and scan the listings. Nobody—not even Charley. I stare at the screen, frustration cooking in my gut. I know from last year's research that Charley was in the 1939 directory, listed alongside Grace. Did he go unlisted? Was he trying to hide from her after the divorce?

I rewind that roll and try the 1962 spool. There are two 'James Smiths' in the Valley at that time, but no middle initials. One is with the highway patrol; the other is a bartender. No 'Marjories.' I take screen shots. Maybe the addresses will help.

Moving back to the research computer, I plug in the James Smith names and addresses. I discover a phone book database online—it's much easier to search than the microfilm.

The San Fernando Valley phone book was discontinued in the early 2000s, but from the late 1990s directory, I find 27 Jimmy Smith with phone numbers. *Sigh.*

I capture screen shots of each name, number, and address. It's doubtful that any of them will have the same phone from twenty years ago, but it gives me a route to pursue outside of the library.

Packing up my notes, snacks, and screen shots (conveniently saved to a jump drive), I head for the elevators.

It's warmer out now. The fresh air and sunshine revive me—I take off my hoodie. I'm learning that I can only stand so much time in that musty basement. And, honestly, I'm not having much success.

I locate a Whole Foods on Seventh Ave. Local beer and fish tacos complete my recovery as I plot my next steps.

C

CHARLEY'S STORY

(1932 – 1935)

1932

Maybe it was the unexpected death of another sister—Mabel, the favored baby of the Frank Allison family—at twenty-four. Maybe it was the fact that Charley had put on nearly forty pounds during his second marriage. Maybe it was the ongoing financial stress of the Great Depression.

Whatever the reason—or perhaps for no understandable reason at all—in 1932, Charley began an affair with a married woman named Grace, a switchboard operator at Rochester Telephone.

Mart eventually found out, gathered the boys, and moved to her nearby sister's home. Charley pursued her and stood outside on the lawn, begging her to come out and try to work things through. She refused.

After nearly an hour of (very public) pleading, Charley finally jumped into his car and drove away, shouting "to hell with you!" Soon afterwards, he began making plans to move west.

Van Nuys, Cal. Looking North. (Wooding Photo)

Charley's family and friends in the Los Angeles region often sent postcards touting the fine weather and strong business climate of Southern California.

1932

Gordon, 18, and Darwin, 12, were each given a choice. Stay in New York with Mart or travel to California with Charley (and Grace).

Gordon chose to go; Darwin chose to stay.

Charley made a quick sale of the East Rochester house for $4,000, intentionally leaving Mart with very few funds. He set up a $5/week trust for Darwin and packed his watchmaker's tools into the car.

Within months of the initial breakup, Charley, Gordon, and Grace headed west.

Darwin and Gordon, pictured with Charley in 1928,
were faced with a difficult choice just a few years later.

1933

Most likely staying with family and friends for a short period, Charley and Grace eventually rented an apartment in Van Nuys. At first, Charley worked out of his home to repair watches, his bread-and-butter income.

Gordon found his own place to live. He occasionally helped Charley by delivering completed orders or picking up supplies but, according to family lore, he wanted nothing to do with the watch business.

*My Uncle Gordon, riding the Allison 'Watch Wagon'
around Van Nuys, CA in the early 1930s.*

1933

Charley and Grace wanted to marry—but records suggest that she had never legally divorced her Rochester husband. Not to be deterred, the couple traveled to Ciudad Juárez, Chihuahua, Mexico, and on April 18, 1933, tied the knot.

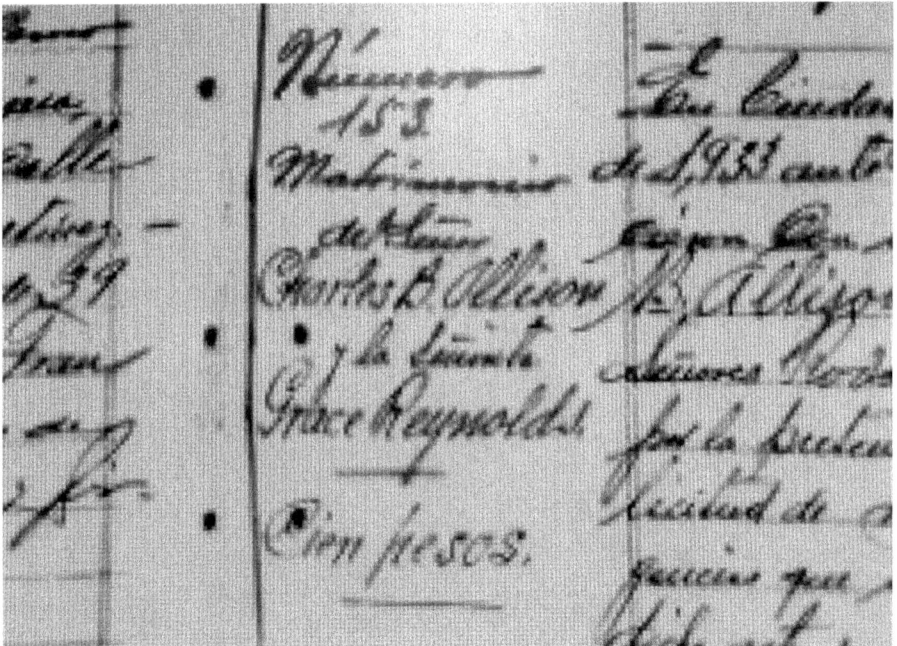

Charley and Grace marry in Juarez, Mexico, in 1933.

1935

As had happened in East Rochester, word of mouth (and the visibility of the 'Watch Wagon') drove customers to Charley's door. Very soon, he had a well-established watch repair business in the San Fernando Valley.

Charley and another version of his 'Watch Wagon'
on the San Fernando Valley streets in the mid-1930s.

G

GREG'S STORY

(2019)

CHAPTER 13

July 2019

That evening, John's family and I go out for Mexican. We are seated at an outdoor table and are halfway through appetizers when John's wife speaks up. "Is that a truck going by?"

Now I'm feeling it—a low rumbling in the earth beneath my feet. There's a rolling sensation, like I'm riding the slowest, smoothest roller coaster in history. The planters above our heads sway slightly in this open-style, wood-framed patio area.

I finally felt one! I know I should be serious and concerned but, somehow, checking the 'California earthquake' box on my bucket list feels satisfying. It's mildly activated my vertigo, but I calm my insides as people all around the patio area talk about the quake.

Waking at 5 a.m., I plot my day from bed. My next scheduled research event is this afternoon at the San Fernando Valley Historical Society. I've been in touch via email with their administrator, Cher (not THAT Cher), who has invited me to visit, but who doesn't think they'll have anything to help. She's already done some free research at the downtown L.A. Archives for me; nothing came up on Charles Allison.

Nonetheless, I'd like to stop in for myself and see if there's anything of value.

I don't have to meet Cher until 3 p.m., so I have some time to kill. I get up, drive to the park-and-ride, and take the morning train downtown. The library is not yet open, so I walk around with no particular destination.

Neighborhoods with small shops abound. There are younger people riding motorized scooters everywhere I look. That's new this year.

I pass a few warehouses. A seemingly endless row of tents stretches along the sidewalk against the warehouse walls. I glance inside a few as I pass. Most are crammed with blankets, clothing; some have books or boxes of snacks. Few are occupied in the late gray of the morning.

I wonder about the day-to-day living of these homeless people. At a glance, their lives look unpredictable and frighteningly unsafe. *What are their family stories?*

Are they able to stay connected to the threads of their heritage?

With no answers to my troubled musings, I move on. A random sign on the side of a building tells me I'm near Paramount Studios and provides a phone number for booking tours.

Paramount = *Star Trek*! (I'm a big fan). I call and sign up for an upcoming tour. I continue to walk and sightsee until tour time. At noon, I get in line for the golf cart tram.

Two hours and 40 selfies later, I'm a Paramount devotee.

I've learned how they filmed the parting of the Red Sea in *The Ten Commandments* (it's just a parking lot they filled with water and then ran the film backwards!). I've seen the brick alley where Spiderman hung upside down to kiss Mary Jane (it's not even brick, just a plastic, interchangeable façade!). I've stood inside a *Star Trek* turbolift (it's smaller than it looks on the Enterprise!).

The biggest lesson I've learned is that Hollywood really is about smoke and mirrors—but, when they do it right, they can make magic.

Back on the research circuit, I head to the Historical Society. It's a two-story, adobe structure with a red-tile roof, set well back from the road. Shade trees and a white cement wall surround the property. I step through the front gate into a round courtyard. *Is this the right place?* It looks more like The Alamo than a community organization.

The front door is unlocked. I knock gently and enter a large room. Nobody's there. On display at various locations throughout, there are black-and-white photos, a wooden chest, a woven cloth, some pottery. *Right place.*

I wander around, looking for a hotel bell or something to ring. "Hello?" A short woman with black hair pulled back emerges from a hallway at the back.

"Hello, can I help you?" I get a sense of friendliness mixed with efficiency. I explain that I'm looking for Cher; that I'm on the Allison clock quest.

"Yes! I'm Cher. We've been in touch via email." I shake her outstretched hand. "I'm not sure we'll have anything for you, as I mentioned, but you're welcome to look through our records."

She leads me down the hallway to a back office, where two older gentlemen sit at a desk, one in front of a laptop. Shelves of brown-covered books surround us. Cher introduces the two men, Jim and Richard, and reiterates that she's been unable to find any information on Charley or his clocks.

I relate my story for the guys. They seem interested, but don't have any suggestions. Cher takes charge. "Are you planning to pull your grandfather's will while you're here?"

"I guess so?" I say. "I'm not really sure how to do that."

Her voice assumes a teacherly tone. "Remember, I do some research work on the side. You need to visit the L.A. County Hall of Records and look for any legal documents: wills, divorce decrees, etc. These are the types of records that will tell you about his assets," she says.

"Thanks, I will definitely check that out. In the meantime, can I look over what you have here?"

"Absolutely. Help yourself," she says and heads back out to the main room.

I scan the office shelves. As Cher had prepared me via email, there are no newspapers, no clocks. Mostly just books about the history of the region. I pull a couple down and get a sense they cover early settlers, not 1950s watchmakers.

She was right. This is probably a waste of time.

But—I'm armed with two new names since my last email exchange with Cher. I ask about local phone books from the 1950s forward. Jim gets up from his chair and scans a high shelf. "Not much here," he says, handing me a short pile of periodicals before returning to his laptop.

I sit in a corner chair and turn through them while Jim and Richard talk about how the next generation isn't going to have the same kind of records as in the past, given that everything is digital now.

Between flips, I occasionally jump into the conversation, lamenting the loss of a hard-copy, handwritten history. Nearing the bottom of the pile, one magazine-sized cover catches my eye: Cindy Williams of *Laverne & Shirley* (I am, of course, a fan). As luck would have it, this is the 1981 Van Nuys telephone directory. I turn quickly to the 'S' section.

There's a Margie Smith listed at 17049 Vanowen Street! *Maybe it's Marg with a 'g' for Margaret…not Marjorie.* I scan to the 'Jimmys.' There are seven generic 'Smith J' entries, but below that is 'Smith James R. 13511 Victory Blvd.' I have no idea if these are the right Smiths, but I scribble down the information with renewed hope.

I scan the rest of the books in my lap, but nothing else is of value. Nonetheless, I have more information than when I started.

Next stop: The Hall of Records.

'It looks like eternity.'

—Mrs. Fuzzy Knight, shop visitor

CHAPTER 14

July 2019

The Hall of Records is downtown, just six blocks from the library. My stomping grounds. The next morning, I take the usual car/subway combo and arrive late-morning. I grab an early lunch at the Grand Central Market and make my way to my destination.

I have the address right but, instead of the tall, brick structure with windows and gargoyles I'd imagined, it's a one-story, windowed lobby framing a couple of elevators.

I walk around two sides and see an overhead sign.

County of Los Angeles
ARCHIVES
Elevators 2nd Floor

An arrow points to the elevators, which only have a 'down' button. The elevator arrives; I press '2' and pray I won't need another allergy pill.

Sub-Floor 2 here is not like the library. I emerge in a corridor that reminds me of a visit to the coroner's office in a TV medical drama. A sign points me down the hall to 'Room 212.'

There's a podium outside the Records office displaying a pile of pencils and forms. A nearby sign states: *Everyone entering the archives must complete two-page request form.* I grab one and head in.

There's a metal detector at the door—and, next to it, a police officer. I pass both unscathed and scan the room.

It's a large space with folding tables and plastic chairs on one side only—obviously the waiting area. The chairs face a glass partition with numbered windows, not unlike the motor vehicle department back home. A clerk stands at each station. Behind them, I spot rows and rows of shelves stuffed with manila folders.

The first window is marked "Information," so I get in line, filling out the form as I wait.

It asks a lot of questions. What type of records do I seek? Civil? Criminal? Do I have a case record number? Who is the subject of my search?

I stop for a minute and consider. In my research to date, I've discovered my grandfather's name with two different middle initials: His draft card clearly lists Charles B. Allison, but his death certificate reads "Charles Ernest Allison." Another mystery I've been grappling with.

Are these inconsistencies the earmarks of an older, less-computerized era? Was my grandfather cagey about his identity? I have no answers.

I know that Cher did a quick search last year on 'Charles B.' with no results. I decide to go with 'Charles E.' At the window, a friendly woman with jet black hair explains how it works: I submit the form; researchers behind the glass will look for any data; they'll call me up to one of the windows if they find something. I can then purchase a copy of any research they find (at a dollar a page). She hands me a slip of paper, similar to a Take-a-Number at a deli. I'm F12.

I find a seat and begin my wait. I'm having trouble getting a cell signal this far underground so, instead of scrolling through current news, I review my Allison Watchmakers notebook. *Cruising* by Smokey Robinson plays softly from speakers that remind me of my parochial grammar school's PA system in the 1970s.

I chose a button-down shirt and pants today—I thought the Hall of Records would be a formal setting. Now I am warm and sweaty after the long walk from the subway and Market. And there is certainly nothing formal about Room 212.

A clerk calls F4. *Eight more to me.* Ten minutes becomes twenty. I try to keep my hopes in check. Will I have some vital piece of information within the hour? I know Cher struck out last year, but I have a lot more specific information now, including Charley's exact date of death, his address, and the names of his companions.

Now Lionel Richie's *Hello* is playing. I hope they don't have another earthquake right now. This doesn't seem to be a very safe location for such an event. I envision floors of file folders and metal shelving crumbling onto my head.

An older woman with hazel eyes at Window 5 calls my number. I jump out of my chair and approach.

She is very kind but has nothing good to tell me. There's no will on file for my grandfather. Her tone sounds almost as disappointed as I feel.

Not wanting to let this go, I ask if she can check the divorce record. I know he was married to—and possibly divorced from—Grace Reynolds (Wife #3).

She says that costs $15 but, if I want, she will look. I agree. When she goes back into the stacks, a thought occurs to me: Why didn't I ask about Margie Smith? Who cares about Grace? Margie was with him during his final years.

I have never been able to think very fast on my feet, with some exceptions. If it's a group crisis (like an earthquake collapse on Sub-Floor 2 Hall of Archives), I'm your man. I'll take charge and make quick decisions to bring the team out safely.

But for 1:1 on-the-spot answers or witty repartee, I am a deer in the headlights. A deer who beats himself up for the next twenty minutes until Window 5 Woman returns.

She's apologetic once again: She's located a 1941 divorce decree, but it's for a 'Charles B.', not 'Charles E.'

"That's it!" I nearly yell through the partition. I explain the two different middle initials to her. She smiles, tells me that a copy of the entire decree will cost approximately $35. "Go for it," I say, refraining from telling her I would gladly have paid $100.

The next fifteen minutes are electric as I sit in my plastic chair, tapping my foot and reviewing my notes for the millionth time. What information will this give me? Will this document be the holy grail to finding the clocks?

She returns with a large stack of papers. "It's actually forty pages long," she says. "Just pay the cashier and she'll give you the entire packet."

I thank her and get in another line for the cashier. Ten minutes and $40 later, I have the first tangible legal record of my grandfather in hand! I scan quickly through the pages—but there's a lot to read. It's part legalese, part testimony. I decide to return to my lunch location, get a cup of tea, and spend some time digesting this new clue.

At the Market, I pick a table near a plug so I can charge my phone. My hands shake with excitement as I set the thick pile of papers in front of me. Sipping tea, I dig in.

Grace is the plaintiff, Charles B., the defendant.

The first few pages outline Grace's request for divorce based on her sworn testimony dated January 5, 1942. She lists that their separation began on December 1, 1941, just a month earlier.

The initial pages have recorded Grace's request for $200 monthly alimony and other assets—reimbursement for legal fees, transfer of all shared property (known and yet-to-be-discovered), and more.

It's hard to pick my way through this report impartially. Charley and Grace had an affair in Rochester while they were both married to other people—while each had children. I've heard firsthand from my father how painful and humiliating his parents' divorce was in 1932. I'm not sure I can admire either Grace or Charley for their integrity.

The next section provides a more detailed listing of assets. I read carefully. There's no individual accounting of the clocks but, under the Financial Statements section, Grace and her lawyer list the gross value of Charley's 'stock in trade' of watches, clocks, and jewelry at $10,000.

I do a quick search on my phone to get a comparable value in today's dollars. The number shocks me: $179,000! I remind myself that this is Grace's version—and it works in her favor to inflate the value of Charley's assets.

My eyes, initially drawn to the numbers, now scan up the page to read Grace's additional statement. The tea turns to acid in my stomach and my chest tightens in on itself.

On January 3, 1942, defendant committed violent assault upon the person and body of affiant; defendant stated that if any proceedings were instituted against him, he would immediately dispose of all stock in trade and property and leave the State. Defendant further stated that if plaintiff instituted any proceedings against him, he would take her life.

I stare at the words, reading them a second time to make sure I have the meaning. *He beat her up? He threatened to kill her?*

I turn away from the papers, feeling like someone has kicked me in the groin. What kind of man am I tracking? Is my quest to know my grandfather and his genius the pursuit of a person I wouldn't invite into my home?

I sit with the information for a couple of minutes. There's no way to come at it that makes my stomach feel any better. I take a photo of Grace's testimony and text it to my sisters, Molly and Judy.

"Holy sh!t" Judy responds.

"Well, we know Charley had a temper," Molly types. "Remember how Uncle Gordon said Charley slammed him up against the wall one time."

Their words don't console me. I sit very still, watching my phone charge. 58%. 59%.

Was my grandfather a wife beater? I consider this, feeling it roll around my gut like a ball of barbed wire. *This is her testimony. What does Charley have to say for himself?*

I turn back to the pages spread across the tea-house table.

Charley's deposition follows Grace's. His lawyer has taken a sworn statement.

My grandfather claims total assets of $2,000—quite a different sum from Grace. I know in my heart that, as much as she's incented to inflate, he's incented to minimize. I keep reading.

He points out a couple of things. First, that they had reached a verbal agreement on November 1 to divide their shared property (furniture) and go their separate ways. He denies attacking or threatening her.

Do I believe his story? I don't know what to think. I take a sip of tea, but it's not sitting well. This decree has thrown me.

In the subsequent pages, Charley makes two points. First, that Grace never divorced her Rochester husband, thus invalidating their Mexican marriage. Second, that Grace says she never worked before and couldn't support herself. Charley testifies that she was a telephone operator in Rochester when he met her.

I sit up a little straighter. That's true! I know that fact from my census research, before Charley was ever in the picture. *If Grace lied to the court about working at Rochester Telephone, maybe she lied about other things.*

You're grasping at straws, my brain whispers. I skim the rest of the documents, reaching the Final Judgment section. After consideration of the evidence, the court fell somewhere in the middle of the two testimonies, granting Grace $35/month alimony—far less than the $200 she'd requested; more than the $0/month he'd requested.

I close the record and continue to nurse my late-afternoon tea, wondering what my next steps are going to be.

Honestly, I don't want to research.

I don't want to think.

After an Internet search on 'Monday night attractions near me', I hop on a bus for West Hollywood and grab a quick dinner before checking out the area gay bars. Multiple cosmos, a cute bartender, and a lively drag show help me forget the dark underbelly of the ancestral rock I've overturned.

At least for today.

CHAPTER 15

July 2019

I wake at a more normal time on my last full day in town. So typical of life—just when I'm getting used to something, something is about to change.

In the shower I consider what research I might accomplish today. One last trip to SubBasement 4? Start calling the twenty-seven Jimmy Smiths at their 1990 phone numbers? Stand on the corner of Ventura and Sepulveda one more time?

Not surprisingly, my mind circles back to the words that now hang over my quest like a radioactive cloud. *Defendant committed violent assault upon the person and body of affiant.* None of the research choices sound appealing.

"Do I even still want to do this?" I say out loud. John and his wife have already left for work, so there is nobody to hear, except maybe the ghost of my grandfather. *Is he with me in this? Does he want his clocks to be found and recognized?*

Do I still care?

The last thought is the one that disturbs me the most. Who was this man I'm trying so hard to connect with?

A steward of DNA that's been shared with me? Absolutely.

An artisan watchmaker who may have had a touch of genius? Yes.

An angry man who beat his spouse and threatened murder? Maybe.

There's no research in me today. I scan the web for tourist attractions. A Warner Brothers' tour starts in ninety minutes. I purchase a ticket online and drive to the studio.

I stand in *The Music Man's* town center. I touch the Batmobile. I tour the *Ellen* set. In the gift shop, I pick up a Harry Potter wand for my niece.

It's a nice diversion to spend my last day immersed in the land of make believe.

The next morning, I prepare to leave town. The divorce edict has thrown me. But one day removed, I'm able to review the situation more objectively.

The one straw I am holding onto is the fact that, in her deposition, Grace swore she'd never held a job.

She lied about that. It's a slim straw at best.

Honestly, I still feel a spark of excitement that I have found the divorce decree.

But crushed by what it says.

I pack my little blue Ford for the four-day drive across the country. Bidding John and his family goodbye via text, I pull away from the curb while my mind sums up this trip: *Can I still appreciate the craft of my grandfather's clocks if I don't really like him?*

Would I like him if I knew him in person?

And, unbidden, another thought. *Would he like me?*

With no answers, I turn on the car's stereo and let the open road lift my soul.

C

CHARLEY'S STORY

(1936 – 1942)

1936

While watch repair paid the bills, Charley most likely began to feel the need to stretch his skills. Perhaps he also needed a distraction from the turmoil of his break with Mart. He'd been repairing other people's watches since he was sixteen. What if he designed a timepiece of his own—an Allison original? Perhaps something that would draw more attention to his business?

In that era, mystery clocks were a known spectacle. Since the 1800s, clockmakers had been designing timepieces with no visible works. Similar to magicians, these crafty inventors sought to create conversation pieces that appeared to defy the laws of physics.

It's unknown whether Charley ever encountered a mystery clock in his travels—but, given the appearance of his eventual creation, it's likely Charley saw a large mystery clock, perhaps in a bank or an insurance office window. No gears to drive the hands. No electricity driving a motor. And yet—these clocks kept perfect time.

How did they operate?

Given how much his grandson loves mysteries,
Charley was most likely intrigued by mystery clocks.

1936

Charley, having become well-versed in the science of measuring time, began to churn over how a mystery clock might be powered. According to family lore, he solved the problem—in a dream.

Within a year, Charley had designed and created his own mystery clock. With no visible works or source of power, The Allison Mystery Clock was composed of two wooden hands which hung suspended on a wooden peg, surrounded by twelve wooden numbers on a plywood background.

According to signs in his shop, while he didn't allow his customers to touch the clock, Charley was happy to demonstrate: he'd grab hold of the hands and spin them freely in any direction, each turning independently of the other. After spinning for a bit (even if rotating in opposite directions), the hands would always return to the correct time—including the elapsed time while spinning!

The Allison Mystery Clock—a wooden construct with no visible works—built around 1936. When set spinning, the hands rotate freely/independently, but always return to the correct time.

1937

With the Allison Mystery Clock as an attraction—Charley most likely needed a larger space to maintain his trade. Renting a building on a bustling street corner (Ventura and Sepulveda) in Sherman Oaks, he set up the front area as a watch shop and created a living space in the rear. He and Grace moved in.

In April 1937, Charley launched his grand opening with a series of advertisements in *The Van Nuys News*. As word of mouth continued its work, engineers and celebrities began to frequent Charley's shop. After a demonstration of the mystery clock, many penned their comments in his shop guest book.

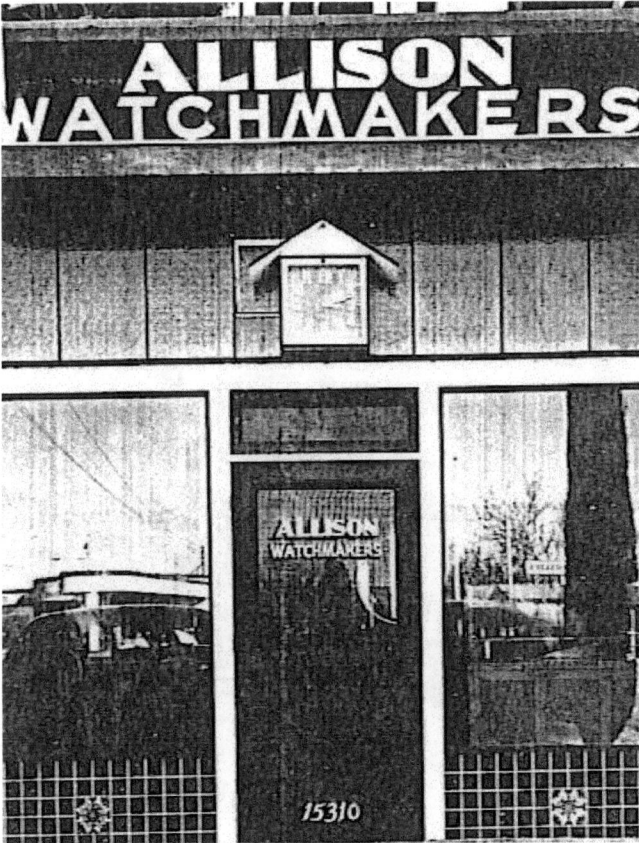

Allison Watchmakers, 15310 Ventura Blvd., Sherman Oaks, California.

1937

Back in East Rochester, Darwin graduated high school as the president of the class in 1937. At the height of the Depression, there was no money for college. With a break from studies, he traveled to Los Angeles to visit with aunts and uncles, his half-brother—and his father.

Though neither Charley nor Darwin could know it at the time, this was the first of only two occasions that father and son would meet in person over the course of their adult lives.

The Allison half-brothers from opposite coasts enjoy a rare, in-person visit in 1937.

1937

In the new location on Ventura Boulevard, Charley's business thrived. Now that he'd experimented successfully with design and construction, the creative juices began to flow. His life's travels had taken him across four time zones. Perhaps he could create an Allison clock to track time in each zone? Using newly available materials such as Bakelite, Charley went to work on his idea. He started with a Waltham wristwatch movement, reorganizing and customizing parts to realize the design in his head.

Less than a year later, his second creation was completed—a daily wind, mini-steeple timepiece which displayed time in four separate zones.

The Allison Mini-Steeple Clock. One of Charley's early creations, it requires daily winding and its four faces display local time in New York, Chicago, Denver, and Los Angeles.

1938

Although clearly "Not For Sale" (as the sign in his watch shop stated), his unique creations went on display for his customers' pleasure—and to attract the trade.

Charley obviously enjoyed the creative challenge of watchmaking. He'd worked with wood; he'd crafted metal. What else could he do to stretch the limits of contemporary timekeeping?

Starting with a Waltham car clock movement, he designed a Lucite timepiece around it.

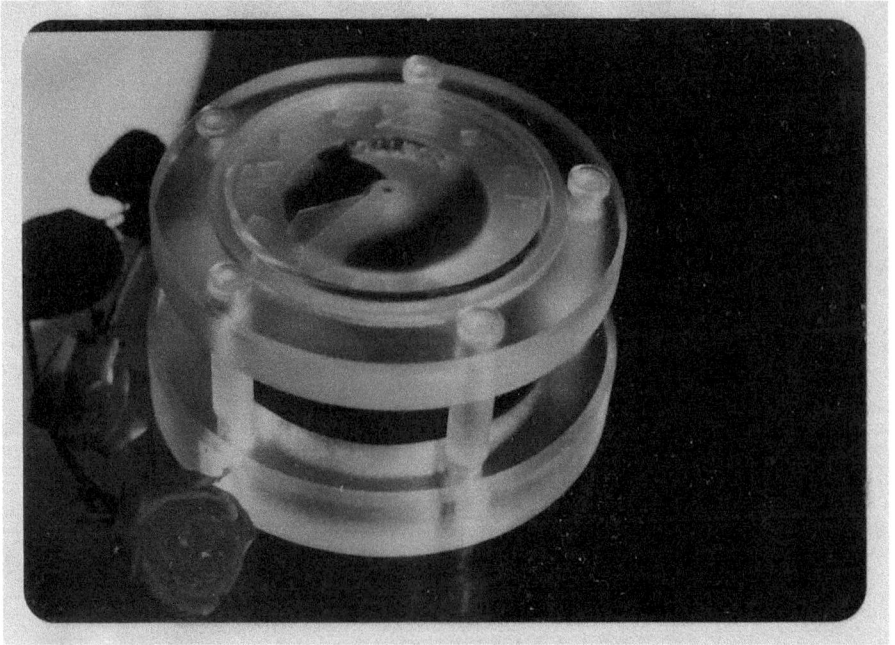

The Allison Paperweight Clock, made almost entirely of opaque Lucite, was Charley's third creation in 1938.

1939

By the late 1930s, Charley had proven himself as an artisan craftsman. Apparently working to stretch his mechanical prowess, Charley became interested in designing clocks that could run longer than the common eight-day-wind models available at the time. While often starting with Waltham watch movements, by machining his own parts and experimenting with added power through gearing, he was able to extend the winding cycle.

His next creation was a three-legged timepiece with an art deco design. When fully wound, it ran for more than two weeks.

The Charley Allison Art Deco Clock runs for 14.5 days on one wind.

1941

While his reputation for watchmaking prowess in Southern California grew, his relationship with Grace deteriorated. By 1940, they were most likely struggling to remain a couple.

Charley seemed to lose himself in watchmaking, designing more timepieces for his collection. As he gained experience, he started with less Waltham parts, choosing to machine more components 'from scratch.'

By 1941, he had six unique creations on display—his latest being the Allison Anniversary Clock. Designed with entirely visible works, Charley incorporated a second plate to house the gearing for additional power. While most anniversary clocks were known to run for 400 days on one wind, Charley's were reported to run for two years.

Like many of his creations, he incorporated the name 'Allison' into the design.

The Allison Bakelite Torsion Anniversary Clock has visible gears that allow onlookers to observe the steady passage of time.

1942

Perhaps in part due to its tumultuous roots, Charley's and Grace's marriage became unsustainable. In November 1941, just days before the Japanese attack on Pearl Harbor, Grace met with a lawyer and filed for divorce.

In January 1942, after contentious testimony from both sides, the court officially dissolved their union.

The court records of Charley's and Grace's divorce are not light reading.

PART TWO
CONFLICTED

G

GREG'S STORY

(2019)

'Wish I'd have studied my Physics, I might have a theory.'
—Frankie Mayo, actor

CHAPTER 16

July 2019

I rub my lower back as I head to the Chapter 13 annual watch picnic. It's been sore since my L.A. trip—at my age, sleeping on an air mattress for a week and driving for four days takes its toll.

Ed has emailed me directions to the residence of a member named Joe. Joe's house is apparently 'clock party central.' Still worn out from my cross-country excursion, I'm not sure I feel like taking on a crowd of strangers. *At least Laurie will be there.*

Since arriving home, I've decided to shift mental gears. Shelving the search for Charley's collection (for now), I've chosen to focus on the clock I own.

I glance down at the wad of bubble wrap nestled in the car's drink tray, carefully protecting my grandfather's broken timepiece. The past week has been one of conflicting emotions. Am I on the trail of a wizard of time or a wife-beater? *Or both?*

I've forced myself to make relative peace with the divorce decree. Bottom line, I don't know—and will never know—whose version is accurate: Charley or Grace. At the very least, I can still admire the craft of my grandfather as I continue to uncover personal details about him. For better or worse, I need to know the truth.

Joe's house is up near Lake Ontario in a suburban housing tract built in the fifties. One- and two-story homes along curving streets, sprouting off bigger boulevards, with no sidewalks but pleasant, woodsy backdrops.

I crawl past the address and see a crowd of people milling around tables and chairs set up in the driveway. Next to the mailbox, a few SUVs are pulled in frontwards, their trunks open to reveal trays of watch wares for sale. I'm at the right place.

I pass more than twenty parked cars and grab the next spot, several houses away. I've brought my over-the-shoulder messenger bag to carry my grandfather's clock—the last thing I want to do is drop it while trying to locate repair help.

As I turn off the car and reach for the clock, something absolutely new occurs to me: why didn't my father seek a repair? The thought stops me. I literally have no good answer.

My father and I were not close. I always had a troubled relationship with him—we didn't talk about many things. From what I know, he had an equally troubled relationship with his father. He was a child of divorce in an era when such failures were considered a shared family disgrace. Shame heaped upon shame, perpetuating its own provenance.

I sigh as I exit my car at the generational messiness of it all. *Well, at least I'm trying to get it repaired now. That's worth something.*

If I'm unsuccessful at the picnic, I have a backup plan. I've been emailing with a watch guy from the Poconos that came recommended by the national branch of the NAWCC. It's a five-hour drive to his shop, but he says he might be able to help me. As an alternative to driving, he's suggested that I mail the clock to him—but that's *never* going to happen.

A gray-haired woman sits at a card table at the end of the drive. She has a clipboard list and a roll of raffle tickets. I approach and she smiles. "Hi," I start off, supporting the shoulder bag with my left hand. "I'm a member of the NAWCC. Ed from Buffalo invited me to attend today as his guest."

"Welcome!" she says.

I glance around, but don't see Laurie. "Can you point out Ed?" She calls to a man with salt-and-pepper hair and a baseball cap, who approaches. He looks younger than I'd pictured. *Maybe mid-sixties?* I introduce myself.

"Welcome!" he shakes my hand. We make small talk, then I pull out the Mini-Grandfather. He looks it up and down. "I think you should talk to Frank. He's in charge of the grill." Ed leads me through the garage, where several tables display an odd assortment of clocks, gears, tools, and more. At first glance, it looks to me like stuff you'd pile at the curb.

"The auction starts after we eat," he tells me.

We make our way to the back deck. The spicy smell of sausage and smoke makes me wish I still ate meat. A short man with poofy white hair and a thick beard stands grillside, holding tongs. He looks up at us; his eyes twinkle with intelligence. If I were casting a movie, he'd be a professor.

"Frank, this is Greg Allison—he's got a pretty unique repair job." We shake hands. I pull out the clock and go through my spiel. Frank wipes his hands on a paper towel and gently takes the clock from me, cradling it with both of his hands.

"Interesting," he says, turning it around to peer into the guts from the side view. "I think you need a watch specialist for this. I used to know a few people locally, but they've passed away."

"I've been hearing that a lot."

He blinks at the broken gear in the bottom of the case. "I think your best bet is to contact the Amish community. They have some great watchmakers. Mahlon Shetler has a shop down off Route 36 south of Hornell."

I quickly type notes into my phone. "I know that road," I say. I actually know it well. Cousins on my mom's side live in Hornell. We get together for brunch at Christmastime. The sprawling, expansive hillsides along Route 36 always make for a pretty drive.

"What's his first name again?" He spells it out for me, M-A-H-L-O-N. "And how do I get in touch with him? I assume he doesn't have a phone?"

Frank chuckles. "No, you'll have to write him a letter." He turns back to the grill, where sausages are beginning to spit and crack. "You can mention my name. I've got his address at home." He takes the tongs and turns the meat. "If you give me a call later tonight, I can give it to you."

"That would be great!" I add Frank's number to my notes. Finally, a live watch specialist, within a 90-minute drive! In my quest world, this is information gold.

I wander back toward the garage, passing a few ladies carrying covered containers of food out of the kitchen. One of them smiles at me. "Joe's just about to start a tour, if you want to see his collection."

"Great," I say, grabbing the screen door and entering.

A man I assume is our host stands almost a head shorter than I am, talking as a small group gathers around him. His thin white hair can't hide his intense hazel eyes. He's pushing past seventy, if I'm any judge. "Feel free to roam around and look at the clocks," he says to us. "If you have any questions, just let me know."

I step into the living room. Every wall surface, shelf, and corner sports a clock. I start counting. Thirty-four in this room alone. Each is unique—and most are ticking. They all seem to be within five minutes of each other. I wonder if it bugs Joe that they are not exactly synced. *It must be a madhouse when they chime.*

"Come see the watches," Joe beckons. He leads a group of six of us down a short hall. His bedroom walls are covered—every inch—with pictures of his kids and grandkids. He makes a point to tell us that there is not one picture of his ex-wife before he leads us to a low display case. It looks like a coffee table with a clear glass top. Below the glass are no less than a hundred pocket watches, all piled on top of each other. I am fascinated.

"That's the Cadillac, right there," he says, pointing to a gold watch with elaborate carving on its case—something like a family crest. "It's worth about six grand."

"Holy cow," I say. I ask if it's okay to take a photo—Joe nods.

As I snap a couple of pictures, I start to worry. His bedroom's on the first floor. There are windows to his front and side lawn. "Do you have a security system?"

"Don't need one," Joe replies and points to a shotgun hanging on the wall over the bed. "This works just fine," he assures us, when we turn to look.

"You don't need a bulldog when you have that," a guy to my right says. Everybody laughs.

"Do any of your kids have an interest in clock repair?" I ask, wondering who is going to end up with this collection.

He shakes his head. "No. My father did clock and metal work before me, and we all learned from him, but none of us had any sons—and the girls didn't show any interest." He looks down; I can't read his face. But the mood feels like tragedy.

Outside, I spot Laurie at a table and take a seat next to her. Right before they announce 'dinner is served,' Ed asks me to stand and introduces me as the newest member. They all clap; I hear one person say something about "young blood."

Ed invites me to share my story. I hold up the clock and go through it one more time. They smile and nod but, as I scan the group, I don't see the usual captive amazement. *They probably hear unique clock stories all the time. Or maybe they're just hungry.*

I stay long enough to eat, chatting with Laurie. When the auction in the garage begins, I fade back to the street.

Getting into my car, I wonder, not for the last time, how deep I'm going to plunge into this bizarre and friendly world. But, for now, I've got a clear path forward. *Next stop: the Amish.*

CHAPTER 17

July 2019

It's been a busy week since the clock picnic.

I spend Sunday crafting my letter to Mahlon Shetler. In a couple of hand-written pages, I lay out my quest in full and suggest that I might visit on a Sunday afternoon coming up. I include photos of the broken clock and ask for his help. To be polite, I included a self-addressed, stamped envelope. S.A.S.E., we used to call them.

On Friday, a letter arrives. Mr. Shetler has written that he is willing to review my grandfather's "interesting" clock—but Sunday is not good for him. He says I can come Saturday, Monday, or Wednesday.

I'm booked all day Saturday so I decide I'll take Monday afternoon off. There's not enough time to send him a reply through the mail, so I guess I'll just show up.

The day before my 'Amish trip' I decide it's time to get back to my manuscript. I visit a sandwich shop for a late lunch and type out the tale of picnicking with Chapter 13. It's a good story with local flavor; my writing group will like it.

But it gets me thinking again about my father—why didn't he ever get the clock repaired? Was he too embarrassed to tell his dad about his overzealous winding attempt? That's the most likely culprit. Growing up gay in the 1980s, I am very familiar with the power of shame.

Home from lunch, our backyard is summery. I poke around our vegetable garden looking for ripe produce, letting the July heat bathe me. It will be January too soon for my tastes.

I finally enter through our back door, deciding to stop in the basement and pick out a movie from my cellar collection. Something to pass a Sunday afternoon.

Heading toward the DVDs, I pass my 'Old Letters' bin and stop. It's stuffed full of almost every letter I've ever received, sorted by sender and date. I'm not sure from whom I inherited this obsessive need to chronicle life. But I've been a saver for as long as I can remember.

In the age of email, letter-writing has gone out of fashion. I occasionally pop the lid to stick birthday cards onto the top of the pile, but it's been years since I dug through the collection. *Do I have any letters from Gram? Maybe she said something about Charley's clocks.* I don't recall ever hearing my grandmother talk about her ex-husband. But maybe.

I pull the heavy bin from its shelf and lug it to the top of the washer and dryer. There's good lighting here and I can spread out the contents easily.

As often happens with my 'archives', I get quickly lost in the memories. Cards from my fiftieth birthday party. A newspaper article from when my nephew and I collected Y2K food for a local shelter. A 1980s TV guide from a family time capsule that, at fourteen, I'd insisted we create.

On the second layer down, I happen across something I'd completely forgotten. When my mother passed away eleven years ago, I claimed a number of family artifacts, including a typewritten letter from my grandfather to my dad. Mom framed it as a gift for my father. I hadn't paid it much attention in the aftermath of my mother's funeral.

Now that I'm trying so hard to define Charley's character, a personal letter from Charley to Darwin escalates in importance.

I read carefully through the glass. There's no date visible; it starts with the salutation.

Dear Darwin,

Just got your long and informative letter and can most certainly appreciate your state of mind at present, when you stop to think of the time and study you have put into the work and the future that it might or might not hold for you. I am not going to presume to advise you in any manner as I consider you have a very mature mind and undoubtedly much more intelligence than I have. I will, however, pop off a bit along certain lines with which I have had experience.

My heartbeat quickens as the sounds around me fade into the background. *That sounds pretty humble and fatherly. Not like a wife-beating asshole.* I read on.

The body of the letter indicates that my father was at a crossroads: to reenlist in the Air Force or start his own grocery store business—as he prepared for marriage to my mother. 1949? 1950? My grandfather skillfully offers advice without being overbearing. I like his word choices and style. Maybe writing is in my genes.

This life is really not as long as it looks to a young person your age. For instance, in another twenty-eight years you will be my age and Darwin, twenty-eight years is a very short time, I know because I can remember so well the day you were born. Personally, I have probably about ten more years and I'll be through, so there you have it. What I'm leading up to is that if you can find any secure position that will give you enough to live on or more, it would seem wise to take it and start living.

My eyes tear. I'm not one who's prone to crying, but something about this touches my core. I never received a letter like this from my dad.

A couple of lines in the final paragraph catch my attention.

Whatever you do, you may be sure I'll be with you one hundred per cent.

Remember one thing: we are all victims of fate and circumstance, no matter what we think ourselves. Wishing you a very happy Christmas and with lots of love.

There's a hand-written signature: *Dad and Margie.*

I stand in my basement laundry as the overhead lighting grants vivid clarity to the framed letter I'm holding. Something deep in my chest feels warm and refreshed.

He cared. He was thoughtful and loving. I can admire him—at least in his final years.

I need to know the date. When was this written exactly, in relation to my grandfather's death? I pull it close. There's a hint of typing in the top right corner, hidden under the frame's 8x10 constraints. I turn it over and tug the fixture apart.

I slide the glass out and peel the crisp parchment from its moorings. A square piece of paper falls out, onto the washer. I ignore it for the moment, intent on finding the date.

December 15, 1950. About four years before my grandfather's death. He thought he might have 'ten more years.' *We never know, do we?* My throat feels tight.

I look at the paper that fluttered out of the frame. It's a letter—addressed to my father? I look at the return address: *Margie Smith!* I carefully but quickly ease it open.

22851 Ventura Blvd.
Woodland Hills, Calif
January 31st, 1955

Dear Darwin

This is just a note to let you know your letter was received and the contents noted. Your Dad suffered a brain hemorrhage which has caused a blood clot at the base of the brain. This has to dissolve and according to the Dr. this is a slow procedure and for the present he is incapacitated. He will take care of the timepiece for you but suggests that you hold it until such time as he is able to do the work on it.

Best regards, Margie

I lean on the edge of the washing machine, grounding myself. I have—just this very afternoon—wondered whether my father ever asked his father to repair the broken clock. *Now I know!* Plus, I've got a new address for Charley and Margie, one I haven't discovered in my previous research. And I've confirmed it's "Marge" with a 'g.'

Honestly, I consider myself a 'humanist agnostic' at this point in my life. I'm open to the possibility of a higher power, but I'm not convinced that one exists. This is a significant shift from my highly religious youth, when I considered the priesthood. Now, a letter has—literally—dropped into my life to answer a question on the very day I'd asked it. I acknowledge that a greater force might be at work here.

The Universe seems to be working with me. Or maybe the spirit of my grandfather is guiding me. Of the options, I like the last one best.

Hi, Grandpa. I'm here. I'm tracing your path. I want to find and celebrate your artistry. Help me.

'The most wonderful thing I have ever seen. I'll learn your secret yet.'
—Betty Matthews, shop visitor

CHAPTER 18

July 2019

I listen to Amy Grant with the windows down as I drive the highway through New York's southern tier. Queen Anne's lace lines the breakdown lane, dancing with the purple-blue chicory in the soft breeze. Beyond, field grass spreads over the rolling hills like a quilt of summertime. I breathe in the warmth of the day and sing along with the music.

My destination: Jasper, NY. *Amish country.* I'm not sure what to expect. Other than buying an occasional jar of jam or loaf of zucchini bread at a roadside stand, I've never met anyone from the Amish community.

I feel weird about arriving without calling first, but I have no timely way of reaching Mr. Shetler. I have his letter on the seat next to me. The last line gives me courage: *Look forward to meeting you...and your clock.*

My phone guides me off the Interstate and onto rural roads—similar to where I grew up driving. The occasional store and gas station gives way to farmhouses and siloed barns as I push the speed limit. There are rarely police on backroads.

A wooden sign, tipped slightly backwards, welcomes me to Jasper. I spot my first "horse and buggy" caution sign. I'm getting close.

I mentally review my opening script.

Hello, I'm Greg Allison, I wrote you about my grandfather's clock. You said it was okay for me to come on Monday, so here I am! [pull out Mr. Shetler's letter].

Well, you said you were looking forward to 'meeting the clock', so here it is! [pull out clock].

From there, it would have to write itself. I expect the clock to do most of the talking.

It's midafternoon when I make a sharp right and begin to climb a long, low hill. Halfway up, against a backdrop of wheat fields edging a thick forest, I spot a large structure with white metal siding. *Warehouse-ish.*

The number on the mailbox confirms that I have the right place. I turn into the gravel driveway and spot a three-story farmhouse set further back.

I slow the car to a crawl and try to figure out where to go. The warehouse or the farmhouse? A small wooden sign on the former guides me.

M.L. SHETLER
Watchmaker
Micro-Machinist

Like something my grandfather might have hung by his door. I feel good about this. Parking, I pack the bubble-wrapped clock into my shoulder satchel. I add my notebook, correspondence, and Charley's newspaper articles. I'm going into this prepared.

I approach the door and knock.

No response.

In the distance, I see a barn. A young man wearing a hat and suspenders is guiding a horse into a stall. Should I head to the house or the barn? No, best to stick with the sign.

I knock louder.

No response.

I try the knob; it's unlocked. I push it open a bit and stick my head inside. There are rows of wooden tables, interspersed with chests of tiny drawers. Tools and equipment are scattered on every surface. Several clocks hang on the walls. To my right, a tall bookcase holds shelves and shelves of canning jars—all sorted and stuffed with brass- and silver-colored gears, screws, and washers.

I'm in the right place. "Mr. Shetler?"

Nothing.

I decide it's time for Plan B. I re-rehearse my speech as my shoes crunch the gravel, approaching a neat, well-kept house that looks like John-Boy Walton might wave out of an upper window at any moment. Sprawling porches on the first and second levels are connected by a staircase at the closest end.

A young woman is sitting on the lower porch holding a baby. She's wearing the traditional garb I've seen at the roadside stands: a solid cotton dress covered with a white apron. She sports a white bonnet. I stand outside the porch rail and launch into my pitch.

"Hello, I'm here to meet Mr. Shelter."

She points in the general direction to her right. "Up-stairs."

I look that way—does she mean the porch stairs or does she want me to go back to the watch workshop? I'm really not sure. I flip through my shoulder bag and pull out Mr. Shetler's letter.

"I'm looking for Mahlon Shetler? He told me to come by today."

She points again. "Up-stairs." Her short, choppy replies suggest that English might not be her first language. *I didn't expect a language barrier. This wasn't part of my script.*

"Okay, thank you."

I take a few steps toward the porch stairwell, feeling her eyes on me. I put a foot on the first step and glance back at the woman, to see if she looks like I got it right or if she's about to call the Amish version of the cops.

Judging by her frown, it's the latter.

I pull my foot back.

Fortunately, another woman, older but in a similar outfit, comes out of the house's front door. "Can I help you?" she asks in clear English. She's friendly, but businesslike.

My chest relaxes and I hurry back to the stoop. I reach out my hand, which she shakes. "Hi, my name is Greg Allison and I'm looking for Mahlon Shetler. He sent me a note and said I should come by today." I hold out the letter like a golden ticket.

"Okay," she says, pointing very specifically to the first building. "He's out in his workshop."

"I knocked and he didn't answer."

"Oh, he probably didn't hear you. He might be upstairs. Just go on in and up. You'll find him."

"Thank you so much!" I turn and head back to where I started.

At the workshop door once again, I knock and enter. "Mr. Shetler?!" I yell. Still nothing.

The whole area is bright; windows line every wall. I cross the room—past the jars, tables, drawers—and climb a short flight of stairs to the second level. This section is narrow, like a hallway. Books and magazines are stacked in the corners. I spot a vegetable garden on the slope outside.

"Mr. Shetler? Mahlon?"

Crickets.

I walk down the hall and mount another staircase.

The third floor. It's extra bright up here—in addition to windows, there are skylights in the roof, covered with gossamer cloth. I don't know it yet, but this is to diffuse the natural light for best watch-repair visibility.

It's much hotter in this area—others would be sweating. I drink in the heat as I look around. More tables and stools. Parts of watches and clocks cover every surface, along with magazines, postal mailers, and metal equipment I can't identify.

But no Amish repairman.

On the far wall, there's an open doorway to what looks like a storeroom. I see plastic bins lining shelves from floor to ceiling. And there, in the center, is a low wooden bench/chair, something like a chaise lounge without the cushy pillows. A thin man is spread across it with his eyes closed.

He's about my age, with gray work pants, suspenders, and a button-down shirt. A bushy, silvery-brown beard covers his chin. *I expected him to be older.*

"Mr. Shetler?"

He does not move.

This is quickly becoming a sit-com plot. I turn up the volume.

"MAHLON?"

Nada.

I approach and gently shake his shoulder. "Mr. Shelter?"

He pops awake and stares at me, his eyes watery with sleep. I launch my introduction. "Hi, I'm Greg Allison, you asked me to come by today?"

He shakes his head and simultaneously sits up, pulling on wire-rimmed glasses. "I'm sorry, who are you?" His voice is raspy, drowsy.

"I'm Greg Allison. I wrote to you about my grandfather's clock."

There is no sign of recognition in his face. I step away. "Why don't I just give you a minute to wake up." I return to the outer room and continue babbling.

"Wow, you must really have been sleeping hard. You remember, I wrote to you about my grandfather's miniature clock that my father wound the wrong way and broke? You suggested I come either Saturday, Monday, or Wednesday, so here I am! Your wife told me to come up and look for you."

He stands and looks at me. "Oh, Mr. Allison! Yes, of course. Please give me a minute. I just need a little air conditioning." I shut up and fall back as he walks to the front window. He pulls aside the sheer curtains and slides the pane wide open. Mahlon stands, breathing deeply.

"It's a beautiful day," he says after several moments.

"It really is," I agree.

He leaves the window and comes to shake my hand. "Well, Mr. Allison, welcome. I'm sorry I didn't recognize you earlier."

I shake back. "You can call me Greg. I'm really excited to be here."

He smiles. "I actually expected you to be older. When you wrote to me about your grandfather's work in the 1930s and 40s…"

I laugh. "I'm the youngest of six, otherwise known as 'the baby.' I'm actually 53." I take off my shoulder bag and gently pull out my family's treasure. "And here it is…my grandfather's broken clock."

His eyes twinkle behind the glasses. "I'm very interested in seeing it!" He guides me to a nearby table and quickly clears a large space. I unfold the bubble wrap and set the Allison clock in front of him.

"Are you in a hurry?" he asks.

I shake my head. "I've cleared the whole afternoon for this."

"Okay, then let's see what we have here," he said, pulling up a stool for me, then taking one for himself. I sit, ready, for the first time, to open a physical piece of my grandfather's world—sealed for some 68 years. I couldn't be more happy if we were opening King Tut's tomb.

CHAPTER 19

THE ALLISON COLLECTION
The MINI-GRANDFATHER, circa 1950

Mahlon dons an over-the-head pair of magnifying goggles and begins his examination. "The casing appears to be aluminum," he says, tipping the clock sideways. He pulls out a small screwdriver and takes out a couple of screws. Under his deft fingers, the back panel slides off. He peers inside. "I've never seen anything like this."

Rear view with backing removed.

Mahlon slips into 'watchspeak.' "This is a Waltham barrel." He smiles as he pulls out screws and turns the assembly over. "This is getting very, very interesting. Some parts are homemade." He pauses and squints. "It looks like he built every screw."

Pride swells in my chest, although it's unearned. I only carry the DNA—it's my grandfather who machined the clock.

"It has a regular train," Mahlon says, pointing to the assembly. I have no idea what this means, but I don't want to interrupt his enthusiasm. "I don't think this pendulum is fake." A few more screws come out and the middle chassis separates. He gently lays the components out on display. I grab my phone and start snapping photos.

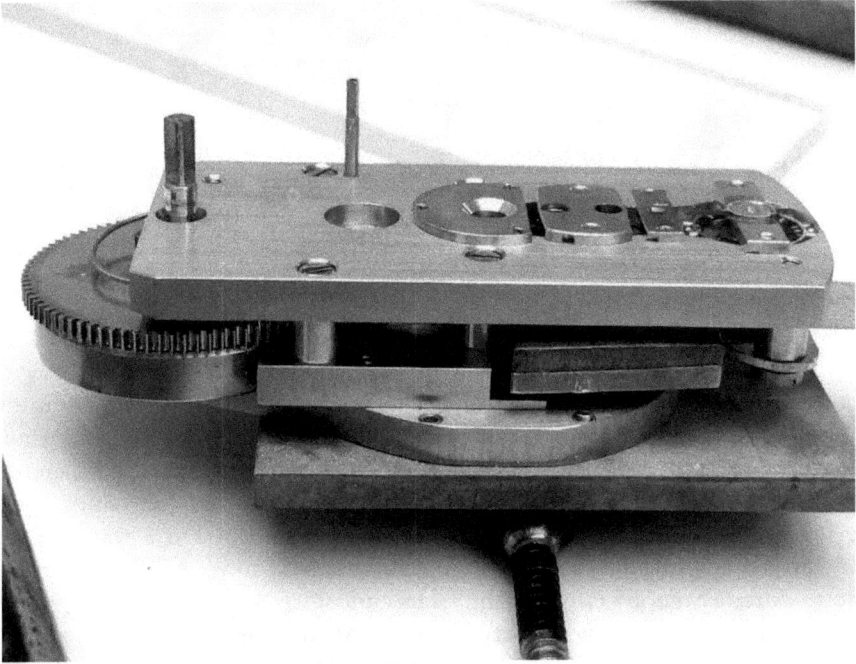

Side view.

"I was sort of hoping there might be a secret message etched in here somewhere from my grandfather." *Maybe a message to future generations of Allisons. Maybe clues to how the Mystery Clock works.*

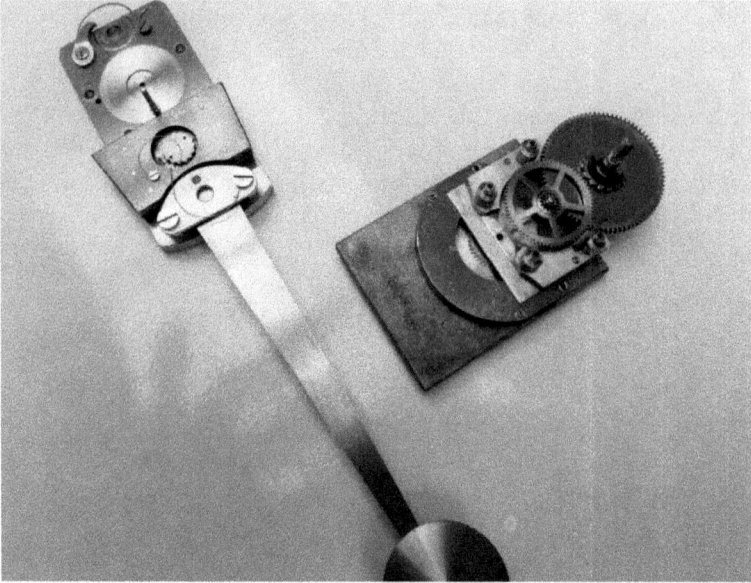

Interior works of a custom-made, miniature grandfather clock.

Mahlon chuckles. "I don't see any secret messages, but he was a little sneaky with this pendulum. Look at that!" he says, pointing to a couple of wires connected to a gear at the top of the mechanism. "This is ingenious." He turns to me; his manner is patience wrapped in excitement. "Hundreds of people around the world will want to know how this pendulum swings. It's precisely balanced."

"You can be very proud of your grandfather," he continues, studying the device without touching. "I'm not trying to be vain, but I'm a watchmakers' watchmaker and I haven't seen anything this interesting in years. The whole thing shows extremely good craftsmanship." His curiosity is palpable.

I feel my smile beaming as I scribble notes. My dreams are starting to explode. *Grandpa really was a genius! People will be interested! I'll find the clocks! He'll finally get the fame he deserved!*

After spending several minutes on the pendulum, Mahlon continues his disassembly. He unscrews the clock face. "Now, if there's a secret message, it will be behind here."

I'm not sure if he's joking or serious *(how would he know where my grandfather hid a message? Is it a trade joke?)*. He pulls the face off and examines both sides. "No message," he says. He holds it up to the light. "I believe he bought the clock face and then added his name." He squints through the goggles. "I believe he made the hands. They're heavier than usual. And they are blued, as are all the screws."

"What does that mean?"

"It's a process that makes them turn blue. See?" He points to the hands. They have a bluish tint.

"But what's the purpose?"

Mahlon pauses. "Sorry, we mostly speak an Amish form of German—I'm trying to think of the right word in English."

94

I think. "Maybe because it is classier?"

He smiles. "Yes...it's classier."

A clock face...with my last name on it!

From behind the clock's face, he pulls out a long, square cylinder with a round gear. Half of the gear is broken off—it slides down to the table amid the parts. "Your father was really rough on this clock when he wound it and broke this." He holds up the piece so I can see it. "It's solid metal."

I laugh. "He was a piano player. He had strong fingers."

My mind travels back to Mass when I was little. Dad would sit in the pew behind us. If any of us goofed around (usually my older brother Mike), my father would snap two of his fingers against the back of the miscreant's ear. The brief pain could make your eyes water. Being a rule follower, it only happened to me once or twice—but I respected the power of those piano fingers.

I take a photo of the broken gear. It probably took Grandpa a year to make the clock and Dad broke it on the first wind. "Can you fix it?"

Mahlon pulls the broken parts off to one side and examines them for several moments. Through the open windows, I hear a car rushing up the hillside road, spitting gravel. Mahlon finally sits back, exhales, and turns to me.

"I'm going to be very honest with you. Yes, I can make a replacement part for you. That might cost a $150 or so." My mind immediately thinks that's a small price to see this clock work again. But Mahlon's not done.

"But, if I make you a new part, then you don't have your grandfather's original part anymore." He leans in. "I believe you can get this piece laser-welded for $15."

I'm okay with either dollar amount—I just want this clock to run again! "Can you do the laser weld?"

Mahlon shakes his head. "I don't have the equipment here. I can recommend

95

someone in the Rochester area who could do it." He stares at me. "Believe me, I'm not trying to turn down work. I just think it's best to preserve the original parts where you can." He looks directly at me. "Then you will have your grandfather's clock working with all of your grandfather's parts."

I have quickly warmed to this Amish repairman. I feel we are somehow now co-conspirators on the trail of my grandfather's legacy. "What would you do?"

He glances back over the worktable, looking at the pieces of the clock set out in an orderly manner. "I'd get the laser weld," he says.

"Okay, then that's what I'll do!"

"Great. I'll give you a contact." Mahlon flips through a nearby rolodex. After several minutes, he pulls out a name and number. I copy it into my notes.

He packs the broken gear into a small plastic container and sticks his name label on it. "You get this repaired and bring it back, and we'll get this clock running again. I put my address on it so, if you lose it for any reason, it will find its way back here."

I thank him and look over the remaining parts, still disassembled. "Should I take the rest with me or leave it with you?"

"If you want, I can pack it up now and hold it until you come back. I know a guy who really admires Waltham parts. If he stops in, I'd like to show this to him."

Maybe it's the warmth of the day; maybe it's his kid-like enthusiasm; maybe it's the praise he's heaped on my grandfather's craft—but Mahlon has charmed me absolutely. I know I've made a new friend. Plus showing it to others might bring more attention to Charley's work.

"I trust you," I say. We spend the remainder of the time packing clock parts in bubble wrap and storing them in a plastic bin with my name on it.

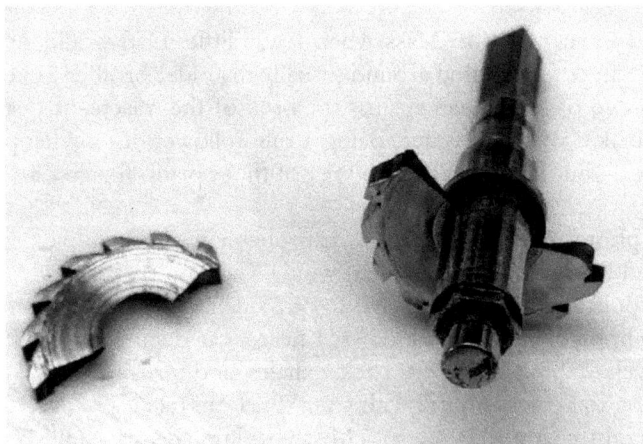

The culprit behind the Mini-Grandfather's malfunction: a broken click wheel.

'Have been in every country in the world and every state in the union.
You are in my opinion the Best Watchmaker in the World.'
—Lawrence O'Brien II, Chief Engineer (Merchant Marine)

CHAPTER 20

August 2019

I sit in the sparsely decorated lobby of Precision Laser Technology in Rochester. The woman at the desk tells me "James will be right out."

It's been three weeks since I met with Mahlon. When I got home, I immediately called his recommendation for the repair—but struck out. The gentleman who answered explained that he had retired from the welding business.

This is one fact I keep running into during my search: the craft of watch repair is aging out. I wonder if it will eventually become a rare artisan skill, like making stained glass windows or repairing player pianos.

One more postal exchange of letters with Mahlon *(sorry! no other recommendations)* and an Internet search *(a few local hits)* has brought me to Precision. A phone call to them has encouraged me—they need to see the piece, but they should be able to repair it.

James is a short, balding guy with a close-cropped gray goatee. He invites me into a small conference room and listens patiently to my story—along with my concerns that 'this is a one-of-a-kind gear' that can't be messed up.

He takes the broken shards into his calloused fingers and holds them up. "It's a nice piece. I can see why you want to get it up and running again."

This comment takes me a little by surprise—I've never thought of a metal gear as something anyone would describe as 'nice.'

"Can I take this and examine it under our microscope?"

"Sure."

James disappears to a back office. I like that he's so polite about handling the gear—it bolsters my confidence that they'll treat this project with respect. While I wait, I look through the clock pictures I took at Mahlon's.

He returns after a couple of minutes. "I showed it to one of our guys, just to be sure." His face is serious; I wonder if it's bad news. "I think we can repair this for you. It would be helpful to know what kind of metal it is. Do you know?"

I shake my head.

"It would also be helpful to see it with the clock, so we can see how it fits in."

I kick myself. "Sorry, I left the rest with the Amish repairman. Do you need me to get it back?"

James shakes his head. "Not necessary." He looks at me. "It'll probably cost you around $75-$100 and it'll take a few days. You good with that?"

I was expecting $15, based on what Mahlon had described, but James seems to know what he's talking about. "Go for it."

I leave the gear and head home. Waiting has turned out to be a larger part of my quest than I like.

I'm surprised when my phone rings the next afternoon from Precision. My gut clenches. *Did something go wrong? He said it would take a few days.* It's James. "Your part's all ready to go. We had to do some additional welding around the base—there was some micro-cracking. Given the time it took us, the repair is $100. Also, your clock man might need to do some milling to fit this into place—but it went well and should work fine."

"I'll be right over!"

Mentions of micro-cracking and milling have set my stomach on edge, but I offer a prayer to the Universe and grab my checkbook and keys. Another leg of this journey is now behind me.

'One of the most fascinating displays of master
craftsmanship that I have ever seen in my lifetime.'
–*Edward M. Welton, U.S. Treasury*

CHAPTER 21

September 2019

I'm on the road again, heading back to Amish country. Mahlon has been busy for the past few weekends, but today's the day: we'll try to get the clock going with the new gear.

A word has crept into my world: horology. It's defined as the science of measuring time and I keep running into it on this quest—in magazine articles, Internet searches, and podcast interviews. I wasn't initially sure how deep I would delve into my grandfather's world, but I feel myself getting sucked in.

Mahlon's asked me to arrive early—8:30 a.m.—so we'll have the full day to work. I pull into his driveway precisely on time and park. Pulling together my notes and research, I knock on his workshop door and stick my head in. "Mahlon?" No response. *Here we go again!*

I'm prepared to head up to the third floor, but Mahlon pops into view around the corner of the building. "Hello!" he greets. "I was just taking my morning walk." (I later learn that the Amish don't observe daylight savings time. I'm an hour early by his timing, but he's too polite to mention this).

We head directly to the third floor. Mahlon pulls 'my bin' from his storage area and we unwrap my grandfather's clock. I produce the repaired click wheel. He quickly allays my fears about microcracking; the weld looks excellent to him and it should work properly.

He spreads the clock parts out on his workbench and patiently talks me through each of his activities, as he slowly reassembles each plate, each gear. I'm anxious to know more about the watchmaking craft, so I take handwritten notes and more photos. I feel the years between Charley and me blur as we trace my grandfather's work through this timepiece.

With the internal parts back in place, Mahlon searches his desktop and digs out a winding key.

"Here goes nothing," he says.

I hold my breath.

The action springs to life after just a few clicks.

"Your grandfather must have used quality oil for the 1950s," Mahlon says. "Otherwise there would be residue. But this clock just wants to run, even after seventy years."

He's clearly excited as he stands the mechanism upright, still with the works exposed. "That is so crazy!" he says as the pendulum swings back and forth. "After thirty years, not a whole lot intrigues me." He leans in, his eyes twinkling behind his glasses. "It's a shame we're going to have to cover that beautiful movement."

The pendulum mechanism: up close and personal.

The clock continues to tick as Mahlon assembles the chassis. When it's all back together, he sets it upright on the work bench. We watch the pendulum move. "It's keeping perfect time," he notes.

"Thank you," is all I manage to say, as joy floods me from the tips of my toes to the top of my head. *Grandpa, your clock is working again. Dad, you don't have to feel ashamed or embarrassed anymore.*

I thank him, shake hands, and head home, with the clock securely wrapped in bubble wrap.

The next day, I print the interior shots of the clock and set them up around my work computer. I place the now-working clock on my desk and sit for awhile in Charley's world.

On a whim, I pull out my phone and begin recording. In four minutes, I've shared the story of my quest, how I inherited this clock, how my dad broke it on first wind, and how, with the help of many people, it's ticking once again. At the end, I focus the camera on the running clock and renew my vow to search for the rest of my grandfather's collection.

I publish the video to my YouTube account and head to the kitchen to mix a late-afternoon cocktail. *One more piece of the puzzle in place.*

C

CHARLEY'S STORY

(1942 – 1944)

1942

In October 1942, with an affidavit from his mother, Charley petitioned the Nebraska courts to have his middle name legally changed from 'Beale' to 'Ernest.' Whether it was a long-overdue correction or a calculated move to leave his troubled past behind is unclear. Perhaps the records clerk had made an error back in 1892, transposing his mother's maiden name for his middle name.

Regardless of the reason, Charley rang in 1943 as Charles Ernest Allison, the name he was eventually buried under.

Nebraska State Department of Health—Division of Vital Statistics, Lincoln, Nebraska

Certificate of Delayed Birth Registration — Under L. B. 22 — 1941

Name at birth: Charles Ernest Allison
Date of birth: May 13, 1892

Sex: Male
Birth Place: Hastings
County: Adams
State of Nebraska

Attendant at birth: Unknown
Address:

FATHER		MOTHER	
Full Name: Frank Allison		Full Maiden Name: Alta M. Beale	
Color or race: White	Birth year: 1863	Color or race: White	Birth year: 1866
Birth place: Orleans County, New York		Birth place: Ingham County, Michigan	

Abstract of Evidence in the County Court of _____ Adams _____ County, Nebraska:

Class A—Family Bible record shows applicant born May 13, 1892 at Hastings, Nebraska.

Class B—Affidavit by Parents, dated Sept. 25, 1942, states applicant born May 13, 1892 in Hastings, Adams County, Nebraska.

Class B—Affidavit by acquaintance, Frederick L. Ferguson, dated Oct. 2, 1942, states applicant born in Adams County, Nebraska, on May 13, 1892.

Charley's mid-life, middle-name correction—from Beale to Ernest.

1942

According to the Allison Watchmaker guest book, Charley met Margie, a slight, kindly divorcee with a young son, around April 1941. Most likely, she had a watch that needed repair. Allison Watchmakers was in her neighborhood. Regardless of the reason, 1941 brought Margaret and Jimmy Smith into Charley's life.

Charley's divorce from Grace was official in January 1942. In a Las Vegas ceremony, on September 23, 1942, Margie officially became the fourth Mrs. Allison.

Margie Lawrie Smith became Charley's fourth wife.

1942

Margie and Jimmy possibly introduced some calm into Charley's tumultuous world. They spent quite a bit of time at a property Charley had purchased, a cabin at the Encino Country Club Estates, just a ten-minute drive from his watch shop.

Perhaps remembering how Martha, Charley's second wife, had welcomed his son Gordon, Charley adopted Jimmy as his stepson.

Left: Charley branded his timepieces and residences alike with the ALLISON name.
Center: Jimmy and Charley pose for a photo at the cabin.
Right: Margie tends the cabin's backyard garden.

1942

Gordon, Charley's firstborn, was now married and had recently fathered a girl. Gordon named her Jeannie, in memory of his mother (Charley's first wife who died from the sewing needle prick). Despite the fact that father and son had developed a somewhat strained relationship (after Gordon immersed himself in religion), family lore reports an improvement during this decade. Charley, having never realized his dream of fathering a daughter, was overjoyed to be grandfather to a granddaughter.

L-R: Charley, Jeannie, Margie. Despite Charley's and Gordon's difficult relationship, Charley doted on his granddaughter (pictured here around 1945).

1943

Charley's creative streak continued throughout his fourth marriage. 1943 brought the next addition to the collection: a miniature version of his popular Allison Mystery Clock, designed on a slightly different principle. Encased entirely in Bakelite and Lucite—with no visible propulsion—when tipped like a dinner plate, the hands spun freely and independently, yet always returned to the correct time.

Charley's American Mystery Clock, based on his larger model.
Pictured here against a world map in a 1946 professional photo shoot.

1944

The next year brought more clock-making. This time, Charley chose to experiment with an aluminum alloy as a housing for his timepiece. Within the year, he'd crafted his smallest creation to date: the Allison Alpha-Omega Clock.

Barely two inches high, the gears were entirely encased in an obelisk-shaped aluminum housing. The face, finely polished, sported letters instead of numbers.

Charley was not known to be religious. Perhaps the Greek concept of "first" and "last" captured his imagination. Perhaps he liked the symmetry that ten letters could easily replace the numbers on a clock.

Whatever the reason, his next creation had a very unique face. One of his longest-running standard clocks, the Alpha-Omega keeps time for 16 days on one wind.

Charley's Alpha-Omega Clock face replaces numbers with letters.
Pictured here with a silver necklace in a 1946 professional photo shoot.

G

GREG'S STORY

(2020-2022)

CHAPTER 22

December 2020

It's the Christmas holiday break and I am flooded with thoughts.

A very troubling year has passed since I posted my YouTube video. As a world, we've witnessed the onslaught of a deadly coronavirus, divisive politics, social justice protests, supply chain issues—the list is long. Fortunately, my husband and I can work from home, so we've been able to cope better than some. And yet, I've lost a year in my search—because, somewhere in the maelstrom, I lost my motivation.

I have worked hard to avoid specific political views in this story about clocks, but 2020 seems to have driven us all to draw lines in the sand. For the sake of the following pages, let me just state that my personal, kindness-based creed supports three "S"s—Science, Support, and Sanity.

As is often my holiday habit, I sit in front of my third-floor fireplace in the afternoons. I like it better when it's snowing outside, but today is a gray forty degrees and I'm denied the comfort of a swirling, cleansing snow.

The winding down of the year has got me thinking about clocks again—and has forced me to acknowledge a truth I've been avoiding: 2020 has derailed my quest. I don't like admitting that external forces can have so much control over my internal self.

For starters, I have been unable (and unwilling) to travel to Los Angeles this summer. Instead, my husband and I have been 'sheltering in place', a phrase that has entered the common lexicon.

Additionally, I've taken a roller coaster ride trying to qualify for a Covid vaccine trial (the concept appeals to the first two of my "S"s). In May, I was rejected for a Pfizer trail Phase One—my BMI was too high. Motivated to qualify for the next phase or the next product, I increased my exercise and decreased my calories.

My efforts paid off. By September, I qualified for a second vaccine trial, having shed more than forty pounds (an achievement I feel almost apologetic about as I view the many faces on virtual work meetings that have plumped out during the past ten months of lockdown).

It's now my annual vacation week between Christmas and New Year's Eve 2020. I've established a routine during my sixteen days away from work—an afternoon fire, a local craft beer, and a strategic assault on my reading pile.

I have flirted with the idea of reclaiming the mantle of my quest. I even went so far as to send a Christmas card and a packet of assorted herb seeds to Mahlon, my Amish watch-making friend. But, other than that, 2020 has left me weary.

I don't feel like picking up the phone and calling the twenty-seven "Jimmy Smiths" that I found in the Los Angeles phone book during my 2019 visit. I don't feel like writing about how publication of my article in the NAWCC July/August 2020 Watch Bulletin hasn't turned up any leads. I don't feel like remembering how the screw that holds the set wheel onto my grandfather's clock came loose this spring and flew off into oblivion—meaning I can't set the time until it's repaired.

So I sit by the fire, drink beer, read fiction, and let time pass.

I'm on Day 13 of 16 days off—New Year's Eve. 2020 is grinding to a close.

During my morning shower, I listen to the third episode of a relatively new podcast series from the NAWCC—they produce an episode approximately every three months. This one is about the Stephen Engle clock, a unique timepiece featured at a World's Fair in the late 1800s. Like many podcasts, I am marginally intrigued by the description but, once I get into it, I'm hooked.

Stephen Engle spent twenty years designing a complex eleven-foot clock—each piece by hand. It features many moving parts and characters. The restored timepiece is a featured exhibit at the NAWCC museum.

The steam of the shower and the intrigue of Stephen Engle's driven effort seem almost metaphorically timed to shed my malaise—just as the calendar prepares to shed this distressing year. All at once, strife seems to exit my life in a soapy swirl. Even if it's only for a time, it's a welcome feeling.

After my shower, an idea strikes me. I look up the podcast host. Her contact information is online.

Back on my couch, I compose a detailed email about my story and click 'Send.' Whether or not she accepts my quest as a topic for the next NAWCC podcast, I feel a familiar excitement in my chest. It's the reignited spark of hope that possibly—just maybe—I will actually locate my grandfather's missing collection. It's a welcome resolve for a new year.

CHAPTER 23

May 2021

Now that we're all vaccinated against Covid, my brothers and I have restarted our 'broski lunches'—something we did weekly before the pandemic. The day is sunny and warm for spring; tree pollen is already causing me sneezing fits.

Mike and I join our oldest brother Paul on the grounds of Monroe Community Hospital (MCH), where he's a resident. Congenital hydrocephalus has impaired his cognition. Misdiagnosed spinal stenosis has left him in a wheelchair. Even with all of that, he's still the best historian for early family facts.

Mike is six years ahead of me; Paul, fourteen. Their Allison history predates mine—I enjoy hearing their stories. Broski lunches are fun.

I select a picnic table near the pavilion. Built on several acres next to the Genesee river, the MCH campus is expansive and lush. Paul navigates carefully across the bumpy yard in his electric scooter. Mike limps a little as he walks over from his truck. We're all showing signs of age, the Allison boys.

I pull out submarine sandwiches I've picked up at a local deli counter and crack open three bottles of beer. I sit at the far end of the table from both of them. "Socially distant," I say, when they look at me, eyebrows raised. Mike rolls his eyes.

We raise our beers to toast the reunion. "This is livin'," Paul says.

It's custom to do a round-robin status update. I start. "So I can't report much progress on the clock search." Mike looks at me across the table, squinting into the sun. "I put up a video about my quest on YouTube and the NAWCC published my story in their magazine." I swat at a few flies who are interested in my sandwich. "Maybe that will eventually get some attention. And I'm thinking of hiring a private detective. Somebody who finds people for a living."

Mike nods. "How much does that cost?"

"I'm not sure. I'll probably just poke around online."

Paul is having trouble holding his sub; I move closer to reassemble the meat and lettuce, which have slipped out onto his plate, then help him get a firm grip. "At least we've got Dad's wedding clock working. Even if we never find the others, Mahlon seems to think that people will be interested in how it works." I pause for a swig of beer. "Can you imagine how ashamed Dad must have felt when he broke that on the first wind?"

Mike jumps in. "You know that wasn't originally the clock he got as a wedding gift, don't you?"

I stop chewing. "WHAT are you talking about?"

My brother smiles, like he does when he's about to launch into a tale. Something he's been doing since we shared a room as kids. He's a good storyteller.

"So Charley sent Dad a clock for a wedding gift. It was a round, clear-glass clock with hands that floated in the middle."

Paul chimes in. "I remember that clock. It used to sit on our coffee table when I was a kid."

Mike continues. "So, when he got the glass clock, Dad called Charley to thank him. He made a big fuss about how happy he was to own an Allison original made by his dad." My brother pauses, for emphasis. "So then Charley admitted that the glass clock was a clock he bought, not one he made."

"I *never* heard this!" I interrupt. "Why have I never heard this?"

"I don't know. So, anyways, I guess Charley felt bad, because later he sent the miniature grandfather clock. That was one he made."

So Charley actually didn't make the clock specially left-handed for my father. This somehow adds a layer of sadness to the whole story.

"Oh my God," I say. "And then Dad busted it on the first wind!"

"Yup." Mike takes a healthy bite of his sandwich and chews.

"Wow. He must have felt even worse than I thought."

"Yup."

We wrap up and promise to do this again soon. As I drive away from my brothers, my mind processes this additional information. In just one lunch, the angst I felt for two dead ancestors had increased fourfold. *Charley sent Dad the clock after an embarrassing misunderstanding. And then Dad broke it.*

My poor grandfather. My poor father.

CHAPTER 24

August 2021

I've recently turned 55—the national speed limit when I was a kid—but, now in 2021, it's a summer with no limits in sight. The Covid Delta variant races through worldwide communities. Public discourse appears increasingly unchecked by civility. Inflation rises past original projections.

The NAWCC podcast idea is 'on hold.' They thanked me for my interest and said they'd reach out if my story was selected. That was seven months ago.

With my savings account increasing and my creative juices ebbing, I decide it's time to ask for help. I do some quick research for L.A.-based investigators. There are lots of options. I skip a few that focus on adoption and pick three whose skills include public records research. I send off emails and wait.

August 13: They all respond to my email—but one of the three, who I will nickname Brett, wants to talk right away. He indicates (with some typos) that it's best if we speak. I dial.

In the first few minutes, it's clear that Brett likes to talk more than type. He has enough general questions about my grandfather and my quest that I sense he's spent very little time digesting the reference materials I'd provided via email. *Isn't researching written materials this guy's line?*

He does, however, spend thirty minutes telling me of clients he's assisted in the past, helping them locate missing relations or avoid jail time. "I pay attention to patterns," he says. That sounds like a desired quality in a researcher.

I'm easily charmed and, despite my reservations at his lack of focus on the details of my 'case', I warm to him.

I finally press him on my one thought that's lurking behind the entire conversation. "How much does something like this cost? I've never hired a private investigator before."

"Well, I usually negotiate a fee based on the number of hours spent. How much were you thinking about spending?" Brett asks.

"Well, I'm not expecting any financial return for this investment," I begin. "I mean, I'll get satisfaction to know what happened to these clocks, but I'm not looking to claim them. And, although I'm writing a book about the search, I'm not expecting that to bring in any profits." I pause. "I guess I just want to help my grandfather get recognized for his…" I search for the word. *Talent? Art? Genius?* "…craft," I finally say. "And I'm dying to know what happened to these clocks."

Brett is enthusiastic. "Yes, I think your grandfather sounds very interesting! And, from what you've told me about his special clocks and his connections to movie stars, I think a lot of people will be interested in your book."

I mentally review my budget. With a year of government stimulus, little travel, and no restaurants, I've managed to save $4,000. *I really don't know anything about him. How much should I offer?* "Well, I was thinking between $500 and $1,000."

I can hear his smile through the phone. "That's just what I was thinking as well."

"How does it work? Do you send me a bill? Or do I provide a retainer?" I know this word from watching lots of Perry Mason episodes.

"I normally charge $50 per hour, which covers my travel time, expenses, and any research fees. You can send me $500 and then I have ten hours to devote to your project. Then we can take stock of what I find out at that point and you can decide whether you'd like to buy more hours."

This sounds reasonable. "Okay. Do I send you a check?"

Brett pauses briefly. "I prefer a money order or a bank check."

My bank provides those for free. "Sounds good. I'm excited about this!"

"Yes! This one sounds real interesting."

I hang up the call, feeling mostly excited about moving the project forward and partly worried that I'm backing a losing horse. *Oh well, worst case scenario, I'm out 500 bucks.*

I go to the bank and get a certified check, which I mail to Brett's PO box in Los Angeles.

August 17: He acknowledges receipt via email. *I am happy to say, I received your funds. I will not be working this weekend and will get started on your research next week. I look forward to taking this journey with you through your family history.*

September 08: I get an email from Brett. He notifies me that my project is a little delayed, due to some other research priorities that have a court date. (Note: All following excerpts include Brett's original typos).

A man's freedom is on the line. I have review your data or the documentation you have provided. I will be providing you a list of locations and the research to be done at those locations. If you have any questions, do not hesitate to contact me.

I'm a little nervous at his lack of attention to detail. *I have 'review your data or the documentation'?* Nonetheless, I write him back that I'm not in any great rush, that a man's freedom certainly takes precedence, and I look forward to hearing from him.

September 17: I get an email from Brett. L.A. County Records is only taking postal mail requests due to Covid. *He doesn't already know this? Covid's been around for over a year.* I'm marginally worried—but still hoping for the best. 'Thank you for the update,' I write back.

September 30: I get an email from Brett. *I am a little behind on my research because it is difficult to get someone on the telephone. I will get back to you tomorrow or Friday with a status report.* Now I'm actually nervous. Not so much that he's running a scam but, moreso, in his competence as a researcher. I don't reply as a test—to see where this goes without prompting.

October 03: I get an email from Brett with a list of locations he will search. *I will be start making request next week. I will send you a status report indicating the documents ordered and their cost when the information if available. If you have any questions, do not hesitate to contact me.*

I'm surprised by this one—he's just starting to make requests? Or, to quote, he's going to start 'making request.' I wonder at the quality of what he'll uncover. I make a mental decision—I'm not sending this guy any more money. Whatever I get for the $500, I'm not going any deeper with him.

October 20: Brett calls me. He sounds relatively excited. "Yes, I've found out quite a bit of information about your grandfather. He was actually married to Margie; did you know that?"

"Not for certain."

"Yes, and I found out quite a bit about her son, Jimmy. He also had a watch shop, which they just sold a few years ago."

"Really?" This sounds a bit odd to me. I've never heard anything like this.

"Yes, and he's got some kids too. He just died a few years ago, actually."

"Great, well I look forward to seeing your whole report."

Brett barrels forward. "So, if you want to go ahead and send me the other $500, I will keep tracking down these characters. I mean, I have addresses and lots of information."

I'm encouraged by what resolution he's provided—but my defenses are firmly locked in place. "Actually, I'm not interested in investing any more money into this project at this time. I'll just be happy to see the data that you've been able to gather and I'll take it from there."

There is a discernable pause. "Oh, well, we talked about a $1,000 worth of research."

I stick to my guns. "Actually, we talked about $500 for ten hours, and that we'd reevaluate after that." I honestly don't detect deception in Brett's tone—it sounds more like he's a little short on next month's rent and he's glad to have my project.

"Oh," he says. "Yeah, I guess I'm mixing this up with another project I'm working on." Even though I'm alone in my home office, I roll my eyes. "Okay, okay, then, I'll write up what I have and send you the report. I got a lot of data to share."

"Sounds good, Brett."

October 31: I have not heard from Brett…and, *finally*, I'm angry. I send a short email without any of my regular niceties.

Brett,
When we spoke on October 20 about the results of your investigation into the matter, you said you'd be sending me a written report with all of the information you were able to find about Margie and Jimmy Smith and his children.
When will I receive that report?
Greg

He writes back the same day.

I have a lot of information to report on regarding the search for your ancestor. I will be working on the report and will have it by next week sometime. I am happy to say, "It was well worth waiting for."

I have not forgotten you, just a little busy.

I wait.

November 19: I get an email from Brett.

I have been very busy with a couple of matters and have not forgotten you. I am attaching a copy of your relatives complete Affidavit of Death, date 2/26/55. This document provided enough information to verify the name, business information, and residential address for her son, James Smith.
I will be finishing my final report for this research shortly, please be patient with me at this time. As of this email, a ask for at least two weeks. If you have any questions, do not hesitate to contact me.
Thanks for letting me be a part of connect you to your family history.

The letter contains the usual typos and (empty?) promises—but it does have an attachment. I open it. My grandfather's death certificate! I was not able to locate this on my own. I guess maybe Brett has been worth it (a little). I look forward to the rest of his report.

December 19: It's been another month and I have not heard from Brett. I finally decide to play hard ball. At least, hard ball for me.

Brett,

On October 31, you indicated I would have my final report 'by next week sometime.'

On November 19, you indicated I would have my final report in 'at least two weeks.'

It has now been 4 weeks since your last contact—and nearly 18 weeks since you received my advance payment to you for this service.

I expect to have this completed by December 31, 2021. Please send me a date when I will receive my final report.

Greg

He writes me back that afternoon.

Yes, you are correct. I have had some setbacks since my last email to you with the Certification of Death attached. For the last week and a half, I have been dealing with computer issues, and I made the repairs myself without loss of data. I just finished the repairs on this past Friday. I am behind and will do my best to get your report to you by the end of the month.

We had to put my mother in a convalescent hospital after a fall. This has been very difficult and happen right after my last email to you.

If you have any other needs, do not hesitate to contact me.

I read it, trying to be skeptical, still wanting to believe. I've known people like this over the years. They spend more time working on excuses than working on work.

Maybe he is full of shit. Maybe these difficult things did happen—coincidentally— while I was waiting for my final, delinquent, $500 report. I am not street-smart enough to know.

After a few hours of mulling it over, I mix a martini and write him back. The good little Catholic boy inside me ends up going with what Erma Bombeck once called 'Edith Bunker-ing':

Thank you.

I am sorry to hear about your mother's situation; I know that is a very stressful process and I wish you well.

He writes me back *twice* that evening.

The first just says *Thanks*.

The second is later—perhaps after he's had a cocktail.

Your well wish meant a lot. Once again, Thanks and Happy Holiday's!

What's a good little Catholic boy to do?

'I resolve to give a better account of how I spend my "time"
now that I've met someone who keeps such a close account of it.'
—Stu Wolley, shop visitor

CHAPTER 25

December 2021

Mid-morning, I receive an email on my phone from Brett, with an attachment. I quickly read the body of the email.

I have attached my final report. I just reported the important details and not a lot of what was research or when. I believe we have a success story, just identifying Margaret Smith and her son, James L. Smith. It puts you just a little closer to your goal.
If you have any questions, do not hesitate to contact me.

So here it is, almost six months after my original request! What will the report hold?

In Brett's October phone call to me, he'd mentioned all sorts of details about Margie and Charley being married, about Jimmy Smith's watch shop, Jimmy's death a few years ago, and his descendants. If the final report lays out all these details—telling a decent story—and includes proof, I'll know my investment was worth it.

Setting my work status to 'Away', I open my laptop and pull up Brett's report. The first thing I notice is the length. *Two pages? That's it?*

I read.

The first paragraph talks about Margie taking ownership of the final home where she and Charley lived at the time of his death. *I gave him that address at the beginning! Who cares? What about the clock shop?* I skim quickly forward.

The second page is all about tax records and ownership of the house.

Brett has researched where Margie lived. There's *nothing* about the clock shop.

My cheeks begin to heat with the depth of my naiveté. Exactly what I was afraid of. I actually think Brett means well, but his slipshod approach, lack of attention to detail, and computer crash hasn't been focused.

There are no stories about what he'd mentioned in the October phone call.

There is little supporting documentation, just the death certificate and a property sale deed. I wish now that I'd made notes when he'd called me and the details were fresh in his mind. I hadn't bothered—I'd expected it all to be included in the final report.

My empty stomach begins to churn acid.

I head back to Page One to read more carefully. Brett does have a section marked 'some identifying information about these individuals.' A couple of things jump out at me, things I'd glossed over on my first, irritated read.

Brett has listed Margie's name as 'Margaret Allison.' Although there's no proof, he's listed the date of her birth and death and social security number. Taken at face value, this does indicate that Margie did become my grandfather's fourth wife—which would entitle her to inherit his property upon his death. That's something.

I look at the next two lines—they list James Smith's name and address. Nothing about his death or watch shop, but I do recall that Brett said in the October call that Jimmy had died a few years ago. Nothing helpful there.

Near the bottom of Page One is another street address. On my first read, I thought it was simply one more address for James Smith. Now I see that it's actually a mailing address for 'Parris James Smith', *son* of Jimmy.

My heart takes a hopeful leap. After all the waiting and all the nonsense, this is potentially a gold nugget from Brett! It's worth $500—assuming the address is current and accurate.

Don't be naïve, it could be old and useless, my (slightly) shrewder self whispers.

Only one way to find out.

December 29, 2021
Dear Mr. Parris Smith,
I'm writing today hoping you might be able to help solve a mystery about some clocks that my grandfather designed back in the 1930s & 1940s.
I located your name and address with the help of a research assistant in L.A.—he's been helping me locate relatives of Margie Smith and her son, James Smith.

The short version:
I'm trying to find out what happened to a collection of 13 "Allison" clocks that my grandfather, Charley Allison, created. Please know that I'm not trying to lay any claim to these clocks if they are owned by others—I'd just love to know what happened to them—and possibly one day see them.

I continue, laying out the whole story, filling the rest of the page. On the back, I wrap up:

So, bottom line, that's why I'm writing you today, hoping you can help me in my quest—to locate my grandfather's missing clocks. My dad always thought they went to a museum, and my uncle thought that Jimmy Smith (Margie's son, and possibly your father) may have inherited them. I've included my contact info below and I hope to hear from you!

Sincerely,
Greg Allison

And, once again, I wait.

CHAPTER 26

April 2022

In subsequent months, Brett's intel is proving full of holes.

For starters, my December letter to Parris Smith at the Irvine, CA address came back three weeks later, 'Addressee unknown.' I search online for 'Parris James Smith' and come up with another address, email, and phone number in Southern L.A.

I rewrite my letter (by hand), again offering three ways to reach me—by postal mail, email, or phone. I send the revised plea on its way to the new address in mid-January. That one doesn't come back—but I also don't hear anything.

Strike One.

A friend suggests I send a certified letter. That way, I'd at least have confirmation of its delivery to Parris. On March 23, I try that option. I receive a text from the post office when it is delivered a few days later—but, in the week following, still nothing from Parris.

Strike Two.

With falling Covid numbers, I've planned another research drive to L.A. in mid-May, this time with another high school friend, Beth. As a recently divorced mother of two grown daughters, she's primed for a change—as well as an adventure. We spend many winter phone calls mapping out our trip.

In my mind, I'll be meeting Parris in person and (in my best fantasies) viewing the collection of clocks (that have been sitting on his living room shelves for forty years). The proverbial clock is now ticking. Beth and I leave for LA in five weeks. To make my dream a reality, I need to get ahold of Parris.

My online search had provided an email address. On April 2, I type an electronic version of my hand-written soliloquy and ship it off.

Crickets.

Strike Three.

With my latest L.A. road trip rapidly approaching, I decide to touch base with some of the alternative researchers that I'd contacted the previous summer.

One in particular, George, calls himself an on-the-ground researcher. Via email, he'd offered to 'knock on doors' or look up one or two specific things. He didn't mention his fee. Nine months after our original contact, I shoot him an update and restate my case.

I check my email that afternoon. I have three messages from George! He's already done some online research in his databases and has come up with an image of my grandfather's 1918 passport application. It's an artifact I don't have.

I begin an email exchange with George. Yes, he's interested in my story (he grew up near my grandfather's clock store). No, he doesn't want to be paid for what he's doing (if it gets more involved, we'll talk about reimbursement).

In the course of one day, I have a dozen emails from George. He's researched some of the facts that Brett provided—and has disproven a couple of them already. My heart sinks a little, reliving my wasted money and crushed hopes. I no longer have faith that Parris Smith is the son of 'my Jimmy Smith.'

I let George know I'll be in town for three days in mid-May. His mom lives in Studio City—we coordinate a lunch date. I'm looking forward to meeting this enthusiastic, generous researcher. And, hopefully, finding a few more breadcrumbs along the path to my grandfather's legacy.

It's a chilly May morning as Beth and I set out on our two-week excursion. For her, this is a mid-life, post-marriage road trip to recognize one of her dreams—walking the stage at USC for the recently earned master's degree.

For me, it's a chance to move my tale forward. I've been cooling my jets for two years of Covid—it's time to get back in motion.

Pulling out of my driveway, I mentally review our plans to drive from Rochester to L.A. (and back). I have so many mixed thoughts. Excitement for a mind-clearing, soul-lifting excursion (I love road trips!). Trepidation about driving through some maskless states (with high Covid levels). Joy to reconnect with some long-time friends along the route (we've plotted a leisurely, 14-day path to include overnight stays with mutual friends). With plenty of 80s music, wine, and KN95 masks packed into my RAV4, I feel ready for anything.

First clock-related stop will come tomorrow—Hastings, Nebraska. My grandfather was born there. It's only twenty minutes off the highway, so I've plotted a short side trip. I'm not sure what I'll gain by driving through on a Sunday evening, but I want to get a feel for the place. And, if a bar is open, to raise a glass to my grandfather.

'To Mr. Allison, one of the most Amazing scientists I have ever met—especially his clocks that have no "mechanism."'

—*J. N. Siegel, shop visitor*

CHAPTER 27

May 2022

In the first 24 hours, we've taken a side trip to Indiana Dunes National Park (where we sit on the shore of Lake Michigan and consume local craft beer) and we've spent the night with family friends in Chicago (where we sink into plush couches and consume hand-crafted cocktails).

Now it's time for Hastings—the birthplace of my grandfather. It's nearly 6 p.m. on Sunday when we pass the "Welcome to Hastings" sign.

"What do you want to do here?" Beth asks.

I squirm in the rider's seat. "Honestly, I'm not really sure." I scan the horizon. Gray clouds are working to obscure the remaining daylight, but shafts of sunlight break through. Old-style brick buildings and factories populate the streets, breaking the long, flat fields we've encountered for miles. The downtown area has a preservation-gentrification look.

"If it were a weekday, I'd look for a Hall of Records," I offer. "But, at this point, I'm hoping for an open bar or restaurant where we can get some dinner and raise a glass to Charley." I pause, thinking it through. "I guess I just want to get the flavor of the place. This is where my grandfather was born. According to the census, his older brother was born outside of Rochester—and so were most of his younger siblings. They took a detour to Nebraska and I have no idea why."

Beth nods. By this time, she's used to my oddball efforts to soak up my grandfather's world. She navigates Main Street as I search the Internet. "There's a craft brewery downtown that serves food," I say.

"Let's do it!"

We park and get an outdoor table. In conversation, we learn that our waitress was born in New Mexico but is headed next month to a college in Central New York, just 90 minutes south of Rochester. *So many unexpected connections in this world.*

The waitress brings our beer selections and we offer a toast to Charley. "For the sons, the fathers, and the grandfathers," I say.

"Slainte," Beth adds.

With a twenty-minute wait for pizza, I want to see the town while there's still daylight. "You okay if I walk around a bit and soak up Hastings?"

"I'm good. I'll catch up with my daughters." Beth and I are very compatible traveling companions. We're self-sufficient when the other needs space.

I walk the downtown grid of Hastings, snapping selfies. Cornerstones date the buildings to the late 1800s. Wikipedia tells me the town was founded in 1872. Just twenty years before Charley was born.

A young man, maybe sixteen, wheels by on his bike. "Hi" he says.

"Hey," I reply, impressed that he's so friendly.

I stand at the corner of town and listen to the silence, interrupted by an occasional passing car. *What brought your family here, Grandpa? Was this a stopping ground to the west coast or was this the destination? What brought you all back to Rochester by the 1900 census?*

I'm not sure I'll ever know the answers to my questions, but at least I've stood on the ground where my grandfather was raised. That has to count for something.

'The Man who, I believe, could hold back the hands of time.'
                                    —William H. Synan, shop visitor

CHAPTER 28

May 2022

Two days later, we're in L.A. We have a relatively tight schedule. Wednesday: Book research. Thursday: Meet with Researcher George and High School John. Friday: Beth's graduation. Saturday: We leave town. Quick, but doable.

Covid has changed everything since my last visit. My mask feels tight inside the subway and my glasses are fogging. I climb the stairs at the Seventh Street station and note a wet spot on the seat of my jeans from my subway chair. *God, I hope it's water.*

There are less pedestrians and cars this trip. Fallout from the pandemic?

There's a sweet honeysuckle smell in the air that is intoxicating. I walk through the park next to the library, noting several homeless men. With my sheltering indoors for the past two years, I've forgotten about the excessive homelessness in L.A.

Back in SubBasement 4, I pop a proactive antihistamine. Working my way to the microfilm section, I'm pleased to encounter the same hippie librarian from 2019. Her sandy, thin hair is much longer now—shoulder length—and has some gray streaks. I feel like we're old friends, although she shows no signs of recognition.

I forego the "Old Chum" intro. Instead, I show her a date that George has identified as a potential source for my undated newspaper artifact. She processes my request for copies of the May 1941 *Valley News* and tells me the film will be up shortly.

"I know," I want to say. "*Remember*, we did this before Covid. I'm the guy looking for the missing clocks."

In the Allison family, we have an expression for situations like this. Derived from a Flintstones episode—where, at a lodge dinner, Fred keeps trying to stand up (to make a speech that nobody wants to hear), and Wilma puts him back in his place, every single time, with the words "Sit down, Fred."

Telling myself the same, I take a nearby seat and wait.

Fifteen minutes later, I load the microfiche reader and dial up May 29. Here's the article about Allison Watchmakers! I've read a fuzzy copy before, gifted to me from my Uncle Gordon, but it's nice to find the source material. I print a hard copy and take the roll off the spool.

Maybe it's the allergy pill (or the bottle of Gewurztraminer that Beth and I polished off last night) but, after an hour of additional scrolling, I'm tired. As often happens, once my specific target is achieved, I start thinking about lunch and beer (which might be a clue as to why it's taking me years to research my grandfather's history). I pack up my book bag.

Outside, the fresh afternoon air feels like heaven on my skin. The spring day is alive with promise. I stop at a curbside Covid tent and get a free PCR test— results guaranteed in my email within 24 hours. I wander a bit, texting with Beth and keeping an eye out for celebrities.

The next day, I'm supposed to meet George at 1 p.m. at a café in Studio City. In the meantime, I head toward 22851 Ventura in Woodland Hills—the last place my grandfather lived. This is the address I got from Margie's letter, the one that fell out of the picture frame. If Jimmy Smith is to be found, this is ground zero.

It's a small, rectangular building with an overhang. I peek in the windows. There's no furniture. Just a couple of sad boards leaning against a wall. I retreat to the street and take a selfie.

A thin man in a Ford pickup pulls into the lot and unlocks the carpet store next door. Gathering my courage, I enter and engage. "Hi, I'm trying to get information about my grandfather. He owned the store next door back in the 1950s. Do you know anything about who owns it now? I found a property sale deed that says a man named Lawrence bought it in 1997."

The Ford-pickup-guy is seated behind the carpet store counter. He's friendly enough. "That's Larry. He owns the restaurant next door," he tells me.

"Do you know anything about Jimmy Smith, the guy who owned it before that?"

"Sorry," he shakes his head. "But talk to Larry; he'll know. They've owned that place forever."

"Thanks," I say, and make a fast exit.

The restaurant, The Local Peasant, opens at three. I glance at my watch. It's only 11:30. I have to meet George back in Studio City at one. I'll head there first and return here afterwards.

It's a pleasant 78 degrees. I open the windows and the smell of hamburgers fills the car. I imagine that Charley drove this same route, from shop to shop, back in the 1950s. *The hills would have been the same. And the palm trees might be that old.* I try to imagine my grandfather enjoying this sunny climate after the gray winters in Rochester.

After a quick text, I meet up with George at the Aroma Café. He's around my age and sports a baseball cap and checkered shirt. We break the ice with general chatter; I learn he's a *Star Trek* fan. His mom is a holocaust survivor. I warm to him quickly.

"So, ultimately, I'm trying to find a particular Jimmy Smith, son of Margaret Smith," I say, after going through some of the details of my lengthy quest. He pulls up ancestry.com on his phone.

"Here's a couple of Margaret Smiths," he says. We look them over; none has a son named Jimmy.

Giving up on research for the moment, we swap stories about writing books. I tell him about Brett and how much that cost. George rolls his eyes. After tea and scones, we part company.

"Let me know how it goes," he says. "And I'll keep looking on my end."

"Thanks." I am truly grateful for this friendly connection after the ordeal with Brett.

It's mid-afternoon when I head back to The Local Peasant. Parking at the curb, I change out of my Batman t-shirt into a button-down. I want to look reasonably respectable when I make my pitch to the owner.

A few twenty-somethings are setting up tables and bar for the restaurant's opening. I approach a young woman with long dark hair and sturdy, Central European features. "I'm hoping you can help me," I start. "I'm trying to find out information about the building next door—and the guy at the carpet store told me that Lawrence might know the original owner, Jimmy Smith."

"You mean Larry," she says. "He's not here right now."

I decide to appeal to her with the family angle. "This is a long story, but I'm trying to trace my grandfather's roots. He originally owned the place next door in the 1950s. Is there some way I can get in touch with Larry?"

She smiles. "He doesn't come around here much. My manager, Chad, might know more, but he's not here today. But you can see him tomorrow."

My hopes sink a little. "I actually live in New York. I'm just in town for one more day."

She seems to read my body language. "I think I have Chad's card here somewhere. You're welcome to give him a call." She digs around underneath the cash drawer and pulls out a black business card. "Here," she says, handing it to me.

"Thank you!" Gratitude washes over me, as hope notches one step higher in my heart.

She smiles again. "Good luck on your search."

"Thanks. It's been a long road." She returns to slicing limes and I return to my car.

'I was more impressed than when I first saw the Grand Canyon.
My respects, Mr. Allison, to sheer genius.'
—Harry D. Earhart, *shop visitor*

CHAPTER 29

May 2022

The next day dawns pretty much as every day in L.A. has: sunny and warm. May 13. Charley's birthday. *He'd be 130.*

I decide to take a tourist break before Beth's evening graduation. I download a driving tour app of Hollywood homes and spend the next few hours visiting Melanie Griffith, Johnny Depp, and Keanu Reeves. None of them pop out to wave—but I feel celebrity-adjacent nonetheless.

After the evening commencement ceremony, Beth and I part ways. She heads off with local friends and I head back to Ventura and Sepulveda, site of the original watch shop. Yes, I've been here twice before, but today he would be 130 years old. It's the closest place I know to be with him.

I stand on the corner and close my eyes, taking in the Friday evening sounds of traffic and commerce. "Happy Birthday, Grandpa," I say out loud.

The following morning, we're slated to meet up with John at noon and drive east in a caravan. We plan to visit the Grand Canyon, the Petrified Forest, and my nephew in Albuquerque.

My last few hours in L.A. I'm antsy. "I think I'll go visit the graveyard where Brett told me Margaret Allison is buried. Maybe something of his info will pan out. Maybe Charley's grave is next to hers," I say.

"More power to you, G.," Beth says, grabbing her book and heading for the patio swing.

Forest Lawn Hollywood Hills cemetery is a long stretch of grass on a low, sloping hill above Warner Brothers Studios. Once again, I'm surprised at how comfortably L.A. draws the line between celebrity and everyman. One side of the road is movie sets, the other side, a gentle pasture of graves.

I give the brief version of my quest to the woman at the gate house. She directs me to a section along the east drive. Within minutes, I'm parked and walking.

Margaret Allison's grave is on an upper slope of the cemetery. Right next to

129

her? *Hugh Allison. Not my grandpa. Wrong Margie. Thanks a bunch, Brett.*

Even though I hadn't expected much, I feel the air seep out of me. I haven't really accomplished a lot this trip. I'm no closer to finding Margie, or Jimmy, or the clocks. I gaze around at the graves, letting the morning breeze massage my disappointment.

Maybe some movie stars are buried here, I think, trying anything to salvage the day. I do a quick search on my phone—and am pleased to see a familiar name pop up.

Within a few minutes, I'm standing at Bette Davis's tombstone. One of my sister Molly's and my favorite actors. Bette is buried next to her sister and mother. I can't help but smile at her epitaph: *She did it the hard way.*

I stand for a long while, drinking in the sunshine, feeling the soft breeze as it makes its way across the grass. It's not my grandfather's grave and yet, I feel grounded in an odd way. The feeling of failure ebbs away. At least for now.

I text a photo of the Davis plot to Molly and head back to the Airbnb.

C

CHARLEY'S STORY

(1945 – 1950)

1945

Darwin, Charley's second son, spent the final years of World War II as a bomber pilot in the Japanese theater. In 1945, on his trip home to Rochester, he arranged a layover in Los Angeles. He'd only seen his father once since his parents' divorce.

According to family lore, when Darwin entered Allison Watchmakers in Sherman Oaks, Charley had his back turned, working on a watch. Darwin greeted him with a private joke, one that only his father would know.

Charley, realizing who had entered the shop, turned around with a big smile, said "Come here, you old son of a bitch," and gave his son a huge hug.

Between scotch and stories, Charley showed off his collection of clocks. Darwin shared stories of the war. When he left several hours later, he gave his father an equally big goodbye hug.

Neither knew it at the time, but that was the last time Charley and Darwin would ever meet.

Darwin visited his father in Los Angeles on the way home from World War II.

1945

Charley's collection included several table-top timepieces. Where could he expand his skills next?

The Allison Pole Clock, created in the mid-1940s, was the answer. Combining metal, Lucite, and rosewood, he crafted a clock designed with its own three-foot pedestal. Decoratively hidden inside the support pole was a three-pound weight, which drove the train.

The Allison Pole clock hides a weight (to drive the timepiece) inside its hollow base.

1945

Perhaps the landlord at the Ventura/Sepulveda location raised the rent. Perhaps talk of an upcoming construction project (Santa Ana Freeway, I-405, eventually approved in 1955) swayed Charley. Perhaps it was just time for a change. For whatever reason, sometime in the mid-1940s, Allison Watchmakers moved just a minute's walk west on Ventura.

In the mid-1940s, Allison Watchmakers moved from 15310 to 15449 Ventura Boulevard. My grandfather has a smoke outside the new location.

1946

By 1946, Charley's collection had grown to ten clocks: the Allison Mystery Wall Clock and nine smaller models that he displayed on shelves behind a curtain in his shop.

Use of a Clement lathe, a versatile tool in the watchmaking world, allowed Charley the latitude to get very creative in his designs.

Charley in his workshop in 1946. From this photo, Mahlon identified that he used a Clement lathe, whose versatility enabled my grandfather to realize his creative designs.

1949

It's possible that rents were rising in the area—or perhaps Charley and Margie saw an advantage in owning a business property. In 1948, they purchased land twenty minutes west of the current shop.

Like he'd done for the brick house in East Rochester, Charley designed and built the structure, this time with Margie's help. On October 14, 1949, Allison Watchmakers officially opened at its third (and final) location: 22851 Ventura Blvd.

Allison Watchmakers final location: 22851 Ventura Blvd.
T-B: 1948 – A promising lot. 1949 – A work in progress. 1950 – A new watch shop!

1950

With the construction of the new shop behind him, Charley turned back to clock-making. 1950 added another timepiece to the Allison collection.

Starting with a Waltham car clock as a base, Charley continued working with the aluminum he'd used for the Alpha-Omega case, creating a miniature grandfather clock. He milled and blued his own screws, created the hands, and added his trademark 'Allison' to the clock face.

While the chimes were merely decorative, Charley designed a unique wire-and-wheel mechanism to drive the pendulum.

The Allison Mini-Grandfather, at seven inches tall,
eventually became a wedding gift to my parents.

G

GREG'S STORY

(2022)

'It is an honor and a privilege to meet such an intelligent man,
and your clocks are beyond small words of praise.'
—Marie D. Moran, *shop visitor*

CHAPTER 30

August 2022

I'm busy at work...and, overall, I'm worn out.

It's been a rough summer. In May, nothing panned out from my follow-up calls to The Local Peasant. In June, I recovered from a nasty bout of post-road-trip Covid. And, most devastating, in July, my oldest sister, Molly, died unexpectedly of a heart attack.

Each of these events has packed an exponentially increasing wallop. Combined, they've left me raw and exhausted.

But life has not stopped to accommodate my feelings. At work, the government has issued a new request-for-proposal and I'm assigned to lead our company's response. It's worth $14 million, due in two weeks. I roll up my sleeves.

By the following Monday, I'm deep in proposal management mode. In my role, coordinating the solution architects, the pricers, the key personnel—and all the other tendrils of the response—consumes my days. Which is why, when I take a quick break to check my cell phone, a new Messenger note almost passes my notice. It's from someone I'm not Facebook friends with, so Messenger has placed it in a separate folder.

Hi Greg. My name is Judy Allison. I'm not being a pain
but I've tried a few different ways to get hold of you today…
I'm contacting you because my step-grandmother was married
to your grandfather and I how the clocks you are looking for…
I stumbled upon your YouTube video about the clock.
My phone number is [xxx]…looking forward to speaking with you.

I read it in haste. Her name is Judy Allison, same as my sister? *She 'hows' the clocks I'm looking for?* My brain does a 'voice-to-text typo translation.' *Oh, she 'knows' something about the clocks.* But years of false leads and the experience with Brett have left me wary. Is this some crazy person trying to scam me? I write a cautious reply.

> Hi Judy, that sounds really cool! Sure, let's talk.
> My email is [xxx]…if you want to connect that way.
> I am bogged down at work this week but should
> be able to find time for a quick chat also.

I return to work and keep an eye on my phone. Judy Allison responds almost immediately.

> Yes, I would like to chat, I have a box of
> really cool photographs that are your families.
> I also have the rest of the clocks.

She goes on to share details about the watch shop in Woodland Hills where she grew up and how she now lives in Montana, but I'm barely registering. One line has nearly stopped my heart.

I also have the rest of the clocks.

Any thoughts of work and the upcoming deadline have left the building. My sole focus is my tiny phone screen and the Messenger app. My fingers tremble as I type a reply. *Don't say anything to screw this up!* my brain screams.

> oh my goodness, I didn't realize you have
> the clocks—that is AWESOME!
> I will MAKE time to talk this week.
> Are you available this evening?
> I'm free after 6 p.m. ET.

I wait, my palms threatening to sweat, despite the cool blast of air from my office A/C. The animated dots in Messenger show me that she's already typing a response.

> Yes absolutely

That's all it takes. Two of the sweetest words I've heard all summer.

We confirm phone numbers and agree to a conversation after work. Now I just have to make it through the next three hours.

I immediately talk to my husband and text my siblings. I let them know not to get too excited, but that I may have found Grandpa Charley's clocks. I explain I'm talking to the 'other Judy Allison' that evening and will let them know if it's on the level.

My sister, also Judy Allison, texts me privately. *I will make the trip to Montana with you if this is for real.*

She's in Florida; I'm in Rochester. We text back and forth, discussing options for her to fly and meet me somewhere along the journey.

For better or worse, I have meetings right until six. This keeps my brain in check—mostly. I'm still wondering about the 'Judy Allison' name. If she is the step-granddaughter of Margie Smith, WHY is her last name 'Allison'? This sounds more than a little suspicious.

I've seen enough Unsolved Mysteries, taken enough phishing training, and read enough about financial scams to be cautious. Which (for the record) is different from 'street smart.' I'm better at 'cautious.'

In her defense, my mind argues, she has shared a number of details that I've already confirmed about Charley's life in California. The evening phone call should clear things up.

When my final meeting ends, I mix a vodka and tonic and set out my quest notebook. I've learned that it's important to keep notes—they'll help me fill in the gaps my memory might gloss over in the excitement.

At the appointed time, I take one long, calming breath, and dial.

Judy Allison of Montana answers almost immediately.

"Hi," I start, "this is kind of an odd call!"

"I know," she says. Her voice is bright. Warm. "I've actually been searching for you for a year—and I was so excited when your video came up this morning."

"How did that all happen?" I'm curious about details to verify this as valid, although my gut is already relaxing.

"So my step-grandmother was married to your grandfather. She was Margaret and lived in the back of the watch shop in Woodland Hills. Your grandfather had a second shop after the one you showed in your video. I used to walk down the alley and visit my grandmother there when I was a kid."

"I know about that place," I say. *The building next to The Local Peasant.* "I visited it this spring when I drove out to L.A. on a clock research trip." I'm leaning into the conversation, wanting to hear about the actual clocks themselves. *Where are they? What shape are they in?*

"Yes, when my grandmother died, my stepfather inherited the place. He actually sold it to the restaurant owner next door. But your grandfather built that store, you know. I have a whole box of pictures I found. Some of them show the store being built."

"That's not a big surprise—he built a brick house for my grandmother here in East Rochester!" I share. My breaths are coming quicker as I try to channel patience. I take a sip of the vodka.

She talks for a bit more about her childhood memories of the shop, then gently eases down the path I'm dying to be on. "So, my father, that's Jimmy Smith, is now 91. I went down to Woodland Hills last year to close up his house and bring him back here with me. He's had a stroke and I just couldn't send him to a nursing home…" she trails off.

"I understand."

"Exactly. I just feel better having him here with me. So, anyway, I went to clear out his house and he told me just to throw everything away. But, as I was going through things, I found the box of clocks in a closet, all wrapped in cloths. And lots of pictures and family documents. I knew right away that they were precious to someone and that I had to find the Allison family."

She pauses.

"So how did you find my video?" I posted it in 2019, back when Mahlon repaired the Mini-Grandfather.

She laughs. Her storytelling speeds up. "Well I brought the clocks, photos, and my dad back to my house in Montana. For the last year, I've been searching online for any information about your grandfather and his clocks. I've had a few of them on the shelf next to my bed. This morning, I woke up and was looking at them and something told me to try again. I searched on my phone with the same search that I always do—'Charles Allison clocks'—and today, for some reason, your video came up!"

The vodka soothes my brain, which is spinning furiously. She continues.

"I couldn't believe it! I tried to reach you right away through your video comments and your YouTube email, but didn't get a response. A couple of hours went by and I went for a walk to calm down, figuring you were probably busy at work, and then I thought 'of course, Facebook!' So I came back, found you there, and sent you the message that you replied to.'

I tell her a bit about my multi-year quest and how I heard about the clocks as a kid. I let her know how surreal this is—that the clocks are actually found.

"And there are lots of family photos that you'll be interested in. I've figured out some of them, but a lot of them are unlabeled." She takes a breath of her own. "When your video came up and I saw the 'ALLISON' logo in the first picture, I knew that I had found the right person. Your grandfather had a stylized way to write the name—I have a wooden cutout in the same font that was on their mailbox."

Despite the vodka, my thoughts are still racing. Will I be able to see the clocks? How many miles away is Montana? What about Covid? Should I tell her I have a sister named Judy Allison, or will that scare her off?

The next words Judy Allison of Montana speaks make me set down my tumbler.

"Of course, the clocks and photos belong to you and your family."

I am at a loss on how to respond. Since I was a child, I've dreamed of the day when I might discover my grandfather's creations. Now, here I am, in real time, speaking to my newly discovered stepcousin (once removed)—and she's just granted one of my lifelong wishes.

This is what it feels like to win the lottery.

"Oh my goodness. That is very generous of you," is all I can manage. No words feel big enough.

"I'm so happy to have finally found you. As soon as I found them, I knew these photos and clocks were precious to the Allisons. I've been working from a black-and-white photo of all twelve clocks in your grandfather's shop—and, even though I had eleven, I always wondered what happened to that little one with the pendulum. I searched all through my dad's house, thinking I had missed it. But then, when I saw your video, I knew it right away. I guess today was the day for this to all come together."

I'm silent for a long moment. The blessing of the Universe, of this woman, of this moment, bathes me in gratitude. I suddenly mourn my faith. In the past, I'd be offering prayers of thanks right now. Honestly, I still feel that fullness in my heart, but I no longer know where to direct it.

"This is so exciting—you have no idea what this means to me," I finally reply.

After a few minutes of conversation about how incredible we both find this convergence of events, she brings up a question I have on my list. "You're probably wondering why my name is Judy Allison."

I laugh. "Yes, I was curious about how that worked out!"

"When I was adopted by Jimmy Smith, I became Judy Smith and I had the chance to pick my middle name. My grandmother was married to your grandfather, so her name was Margaret Allison. I decided to take her last name as my middle name."

"Later I was married and divorced. After that, I wanted to become a real estate agent, but I didn't want to go back to a generic name like Judy Smith. So I decided to go with my first and middle name."

Mystery solved. I've warmed exponentially to her in the course of this conversation, and now feel comfortable sharing one of the freaky coincidences about all this. "I hope this doesn't sound too weird, but I actually have a sister whose name is Judy Allison. So there's actually two Judy Allisons involved with this."

Judy from Montana laughs. All tension leaves my body. I haven't scared her away. My dream is really coming true.

She describes each of the clocks for me and promises to text me pictures later. One thing becomes quickly apparent—she has the smaller American Mystery Clock my dad told me about, but not the big Allison Mystery Clock.

When there's a pause, I jump in. "Any chance you've seen a larger clock— something on a plywood board with hands that spin or can be removed? When I was little, my dad told me about the Allison Mystery Clock. It was apparently a pretty big deal." I hold my breath.

"I'm sorry, I haven't seen anything like that."

My heart sinks a bit, but not much. I'm too excited to feel bad right now. *I'll keep looking for the big mystery clock later.* "I'm still in touch with the people who bought my dad's house in L.A. I can ask them to look through the garage and attic again."

"That would be wonderful. Thank you!"

The conversation goes on for another hour as we swap stories about our family lineage. We finally get around to logistics.

"How do you want to get the clocks?"

"Well," my brain continues its churn. "I don't want you to ship them. They are irreplaceable. I guess I'll drive out." I plug our addresses into my map app and figure out that it's a 32-hour drive from Rochester to the Bitter Root Valley. "Give me some time to figure it out. Let me check my work schedule and I'll text you with a game plan."

She agrees and we wrap up. Once the phone is down, I rush to tell my husband the exciting news.

'God has given you a gift that no other person on this earth possesses.'
—Lucy Campbell, shop visitor

CHAPTER 31

September 2022

A lot happens in the next seven days that makes it one of the most stressful periods of my life.

First: my 32-hour drive—one way. The back of my mind runs 'worst-case scenarios' against my will. *What if she changes her mind? What if I have a car crash before I leave? What if her 91-year-old father dies this week?*

Second: work is extremely busy, but the proposal submission deadline is just days away. I focus on early September. Labor Day weekend. This seems like the right fit. I can do the drive in two 10-hour days and one 12-hour day. Three days out, three days back. If I leave on Wednesday, I can be there and back by the following Wednesday.

I submit my work request for time off, then text my siblings. My sister Judy and I work out a plan. She'll fly to Billings, Montana and join me Friday evening. On the return, she'll drive with me through Chicago, where she'll catch a plane home on Monday morning. It's a tight timeline, but it's doable. She books her flights.

In bed, I find it hard to fall asleep. My mind alternates between disaster scenarios (*Ten-Vehicle Pile-up Destroys Rare Clock Collection*) and grandiose future possibilities (*Documentary Filmmaker Selects Best-selling Memoir For Next Project*). In the morning, I'm tired but happy.

The first real snag comes from work. The government extends the proposal deadline by a week—overlapping with my road trip. This opens a can of worms. From past experience, I know this will cause us to second-guess every inch of our 100+ page response. It adds complexity to my drive.

I talk it over with my manager. I agree to be available by phone. We identify a backup resource to be "hands on keyboard" in my absence, if needed.

To keep my relatives sorted properly, I begin referring to my new stepcousin as 'Judy Montana' and my sister, 'Judy Florida.' We trade a few texts through the weekend, talking about trip logistics and clock stories.

I ask Judy Montana if she'd like to see anything from my own Charley collection. She wants to see the Mini-Grandfather and the shop book. I pack both in bubble wrap.

On the appointed Wednesday, I load the car while taking work meetings through my ear buds. It's complicated, but I'm good at multi-tasking. I've made sure empty rubber bins, tissue paper, and bubble wrap are in plentiful supply— everything I'll need to pack sensitive clocks for a 1500-mile journey.

Over my lunch hour, I drive to a few stores picking up our best local cheesecake and driest local wine. I want to give Judy Montana a gift from my area.

It's around three o'clock when my husband helps me carry the last bits of luggage to my solidly packed RAV4. "Good luck on your quest," he says, kissing me goodbye.

"Thanks," I reply, hugging him tight, knowing this is the last I'll touch him for the next two weeks. When I return, I'll quarantine in the guest room for five days, to be Covid-safe.

I continue to take meetings from the car. Traffic is light. I'm driving into the sun, but it doesn't bother me because I'm heading toward the prize. After sunset, a crescent moon tracks with me out my driver's window. It reminds me of a story my sister Judy told me about Charley when I was a kid.

One evening, my grandfather was driving unfamiliar Upstate New York backroads during the 1920s—and got lost. With no GPS or map app available to him, he pulled the car over, got out, and located the North Star in the night sky. This gave him the direction he needed to find his way home.

I am tired after a full day at work—but I'm also able to channel my "inner Allison"—a reservoir of steely determination that helps me be hyper-effective when I need to be.

I've seen it in my father—who, in the 1960s, purchased a backhoe, bull dozer, and dump truck and, through sheer grit, built a fifty-lot mobile home park on an empty field he'd purchased.

I've seen it in my handicapped older brother, Paul, mostly confined to a wheelchair/scooter, but who nonetheless continues to fight his way through physical therapy, just to advance a few steps across the room.

And now, it helps me stay alert at the wheel as I put in eight road hours on opening night, reaching Freemont, Indiana. First leg done.

Comfortable in my hotel bed, my thoughts turn to my dad. What would he think about me locating his father's collection? It surprises me that I've never mentally explored this. I drift off, deciding that, if he were Drinking Dad, he'd 'express fascination at this extraordinary turn of events.' If he were not drinking, he'd probably call it 'a hell of a find!' Either way, I know in my heart it's a win.

The next morning, my calf muscles are stiff from the previous day's drive. After showering and dressing, I do some stretches to limber up (as limber as 56 gets). I check out and head to the car. Clock and shop book are right where I left them, wrapped in bubble wrap in the storage area at the back of my SUV. *What was I thinking, leaving them in the car overnight?* I mentally kick myself, although it's turned out fine.

I'm on the road in time for an 8 a.m. dial-in meeting. I take a huge bite from my complimentary hotel apple—and immediately spit out the dark-colored core, rotten and soggy. *Yuck.* If I were a superstitious person, I'd take this as a bad sign.

I ease on through the morning and into the afternoon, passing bodies of water on both sides of the highway. There are no signs, so I wonder if they're ponds, lakes, or wetlands. Seconds later, I cross a huge bridge—this one does have a sign. *Mississippi River.*

I drink it in, thinking of Huck Finn and riverboats.

Now in Minnesota, I dial up some Garrison Keillor Lake Wobegon stories on my cell phone. As his low, melodious voice carries me along, I look out across the fertile fields. Rows of wheat stalks bend in the wind, as if parting in deference to the gravity of my quest. White-capped lilies of the valley line the highway, gifting me a landscape of beauty as I travel.

Making it to a Mitchell, SD hotel room, I briefly log into my work laptop and catch up on email. A beer and a new episode of *The Rings of Power* help me wind down.

Friday waking is a little rough. I haven't slept well. I review my schedule and decide this will be an easier day. I only have an eight-hour drive to Billings, where I'll meet up with my sister. I only have two meetings to dial into. *Piece of cake.*

The signs for Wall Drug 'as featured in USA Today, Reader's Digest, and on Good Morning America' assail me for more than a hundred miles. When I approach the exit, I'm unable to resist a stop. With its multiple kitschy stores and prolific Laura Ingalls memorabilia, it actually lives up to the hype. I pick up a book and some fudge.

Around noon, I pass the "Welcome to Montana" sign. *I'm now in the same state as the clocks!* I stop for a selfie.

My phone leads me off the Interstate and down a rural, two-lane highway. The app assures me it's a faster route. I'm sometimes skeptical about such detours but, as yellow flowers begin to hug the road, drawing my view to the vast backdrop of craggy hillsides, I relax into the experience.

I arrive in Billings around dinnertime, two hours before my sister's plane is due to land. I check into the hotel and collapse into bed for a thirty-minute nap. After which, I check my work email. BIG mistake.

There's been a significant setback in the proposal response—one of the key personnel has quit. It's a big deal, this far into the process. One more thing to cope with. I stay on my laptop until it's time to head to the airport.

My reliable sister arrives as scheduled. She sports wavy gray locks and has a solid frame (not unlike my own). When we were young, people sometimes thought we were twins.

I set all thoughts of work aside. We spend the rest of the night talking clocks and drinking beer.

Saturday is clock day. It's already power-packed, with a six-hour drive to Judy Montana's house, then a six-hour drive back to Billings. We plot that we can visit with our newly found stepcousin for a maximum of three hours. It's tight, but it should work.

Mid-morning, I'm in the rider's seat on the phone with my boss, trying to sort out the key personnel issue. Cell service is sketchy out here, but I've got a solid three bars at the moment.

During the conversation, he takes a look at our PowerPoint proposal and questions the compliance of our graphics. My heart sinks—this can be another showstopper and we have lots of graphics on the thirty-plus slides. And my backup is on a sailboat today, out of range.

My insides wind up. *Not this weekend. This is my clock weekend. The end of a search that started when I was a kid. I want to think about the journey that's brought me here, not the font size in our PowerPoint graphics.*

I get my laptop online via my cell phone hot spot and schedule an 'emergency Saturday call' with the proposal team at the top of the hour. My sister exits Interstate 90 onto a two-lane backroad that will take us to our stepcousin's town.

I begin texting members of the team to make them aware of the upcoming meeting (it is, after all, Labor Day weekend! Who will be checking their work email on Saturday afternoon??). I'm on my fourth text when a 'message failed to send' notification pops up. I glance at my phone. *Zero bars.*

Fuck!! "I'm so sorry to say this but we need to turn around!" I say to my sister, holding my voice as steady as I can. My hands have started to shake.

At work and among friends, I'm known as a "doer." I facilitate high-powered meetings; I throw themed parties; I've helped plan weddings. My annual review always includes some version of the sentiment: *Greg is adept at coordinating multiple efforts simultaneously.*

In general, I can take on a lot and roll with it. Multi-tasking revs me up.

And yet.

At this point in the drive, we're barreling toward the Beaverhead-Deerlodge National Forest and Judy Montana's house. There's very little shoulder, but there's also no traffic. Judy Florida makes an efficient K-turn and we circle back for about a mile to where I have two bars of cell signal. She finds a pull-off and we park.

"What do you want to do?" she says.

"I don't know, I don't know," I stutter out, trying to pull up my map app, trying to get a frame of reference.

"It's off-highway driving whether we take the northern or southern route to her house," my sister adds. Her steady tone calms me.

"I just…" I start, wanting to rant at the top of my lungs, like our dad used to do. I try to rein in my anger. "I just want today to fucking be about the clocks, not about this fucking work project." Swearing helps relieve the pressure.

"I mean, I've been looking for these fucking clocks for five years. And I just want to enjoy this day for that. For Charley. For all of us. Not be on a fucking meeting," I shake the phone at her, tugging one of the ear buds from my ear. "Not be on a fucking laptop trying to solve some fucking problem about fucking graphic font sizes!"

It's actually fouler language than my dad ever used, but it feels good. My sister doesn't need explanation, she knows me well. Her voice carries support without judgment. "Well, we can stay right here for your call if you want."

I look at the clock. The emergency meeting doesn't start for twenty minutes. Twenty minutes we'll lose from an already narrow window at Judy Montana's house—not to mention however long the meeting itself takes. "No. I don't want to interrupt our time with the clocks."

We sit for a minute and my mind spins. As much as I like to control things, the Universe is working against me on this one. We talk it through. I decide to call the project's solution architect and relinquish control to her. In this case, it's about me learning to *let go*.

One quick phone call later and we're back on the road.

"You know what," I say to my sister, gazing out at the deep blue sky, stretching wide in every direction. Fir trees pepper the landscape, accented by gentle slopes and sculpted, pointy mountains. "Maybe the Universe is actually working *with me* on this one."

We reach my stepcousin's town just after lunch. We've had a snack in the car; I don't want to show up ravenous. I have a cell signal again, but I refrain from checking work email. "This is clock time now," I say to my sister, although I'm actually saying it to reaffirm my release of control.

The sky has lost its brilliance. Instead, a gray haze hangs in the air, reminding me of cloudy January days in Rochester. Our hostess has prepared us for this— there are wildfires in the mountains to the east and west, which have choked the Bitter Root Valley.

"There's no danger of fire," she let me know a couple of days ago. "But it makes our air yucky. Hopefully you're not super sensitive to that. And I'm sorry you won't be able to see our beautiful valley with the typical blue sky."

With restored cell service, I decide to text Judy Montana about recording our arrival on video. I don't want to spoil the moment, but part of me thinks that this could be a documentary someday.

> hi—dumb question from me…when we first arrive,
> I'm torn between having the video on to "capture the moment"…
> versus leaving the video off just so we can enjoy the moment
> as people. Do you have an opinion/preference?

She writes back almost immediately. I quickly learn that my newfound cousin and I are on the same page about this stuff.

Actually, I think that's a good question.
But I'm fine with the video. I say do it.
You don't have to use it if you don't like it.
Just make sure I look good. Lol.

I am starting to love her even before meeting her in person.

We navigate the side streets. It has a standard small-town feel: tree-lined lanes with ubiquitous sidewalks. Faster than I expect, we are at our destination: Judy Montana's driveway. It's actually more of a parking lot—an expansive chunk of pavement to our right; a modest, white house to our left. It looks like a one-room schoolhouse. A metal mesh fence surrounds the property. A lone chicken grazes in the yard.

We are *here*. The convergence of Charley's world in the west and my world in the east, with the clocks at center stage. I take a deep breath.

A woman who I assume is Judy Montana leans on the fence. Through the windshield, I wave—she waves back.

We park and gather ourselves. I put Judy Florida in charge of video duty. Judy Montana opens her gate and approaches. I hop out and head toward her. She's shorter than I am, a slender woman with shoulder-length dark hair. In the strength of her nose and her long, attractive face, I spot hints of the Lebanese heritage she's told me about. She's smaller than any Allisons I've known; jeans hug her thin legs and hips.

We hug, more awkwardly than I had envisioned in my mind.

"Welcome travelers," she says. Her smile is wide. We walk up her sidewalk, making small talk about our route to get here, about not needing to lock the car in her town. She is clearly proud of her home.

"It was a Christian Science church when I bought it," she says. "I've remodeled the basement as an apartment for my granddaughter, her husband, and my great-grandson."

"Wow," I say. *She doesn't look old enough to have grandchildren, much less great-grandchildren!*

"How long do I need to video?" Judy Florida, my ever-practical sister, asks.

"Just until we see the clocks is okay," I direct.

We step across the threshold and into the expansive main room—it's unlike any home I've been in. Judy Montana has selected a unique space. Maybe she's also channeling a bit of her step-grandfather's creative energy.

"This is beautiful!" I say, taking a quick look at the original, preserved woodwork, the breakfast bar with stools, the wall of windows. But my attention almost immediately zeroes in on the kitchen table—a wooden, oversized slab filling the center of the room. Eleven clocks are set out on display.

"Oh my God, the clocks!" I say, feeling the enormity of the event—but also feeling the eyes of the video camera.

It's tough to be me. I experience life deeply—but, in the moment, my mind thinks forward to a potential documentary special. *Ken Burns could be interested. Stuff happens.*

"They're so small!" I add. "They looked so big in the pictures!"

My hand briefly covers my mouth as I try to find the moment. My brain has been swirling with extended government deadlines, lack of cell phone coverage, dubious research assistants, and YouTube videos. All of this has led me here.

I'm here. These are Charley's clocks. For all intents and purposes, the quest is complete.

Judy Montana breaks the silence. "This is my dad, Jimmy Smith," she says as an elderly man in a white t-shirt and suspenders emerges from a left-hand alcove. He uses a walker to approach us. "He remembers your Uncle Gordon," she adds. "This is Greg," she tells him.

"Does he mind if he's in the video?" my sister asks.

"It's okay," she replies.

"Mr. Smith!" I raise my voice, in case he's hard of hearing. I approach and extend my hand. "I'm Gordon's nephew." He shakes.

His smile is as warm as his stepdaughter's. She's prepared me that he's suffered a stroke and has trouble communicating. I mention my cousin Jeannie, Gordon's daughter, who I've seen in photos with Jimmy. His face clouds and he looks at his daughter. "I don't remember," he says. I decide to let that go.

"Okay. But you knew my grandpa, Charley."

"Oh yeah," he says, his face brightening. We're obviously on more familiar ground. "He built the uhh…."

"Watch store?"

"Oh yeah. And because I, uhh, lived with him."

I immediately like Jimmy Smith. He's literally the only living connection to my grandfather. I want to know so much from this man who has difficulty expressing his thoughts.

Unbidden, the words of the Grace Reynolds divorce decree ring inside my head. *Defendant further stated that if plaintiff instituted any proceedings against him he would take her life.*

I push forward. "And your daughter tells me you called him 'Dad'," I add, watching his reaction.

He looks directly into my eyes. "Yeah!"

I press. "So, was good to you?"

His tone is sharp and clear. "Oh, yeah!"

His words melt my heart. *Charley was kind to him. I'd be able to tell if he was lying.* This aging man, who struggles to string a full sentence together, has given my grandfather a hearty endorsement. A slim shaft of light shines through the cloud of doubt that's plagued me for more than three years.

Every life is complicated.

Every story has layers.

We turn to the table. Judy Montana holds up each of the clocks for us, telling us where she's kept them, which ones have been occasionally ticking. My sister and I make a few comments. When Judy sets the last one back on the table, Jimmy gestures. "Plywood...uhh, plywood," he says.

My heart skips a beat. "Judy, I think he's talking about the big mystery clock. Did you hear anything back from the people that bought his house?"

"I'm sorry," she says. "They looked all around and didn't find it." I wrestle with this, but just for a moment. There's too much joy to be had.

Oh well—at least I have the little one! Dad told me it worked on the same principle. Mahlon and I still have a shot to figure out Charley's dreamed-of design.

We sit down at the table and begin to turn through the box of pictures. I recognize photos of my father, Uncle Gordon, my grandmother, and Charley in various locations around East Rochester. This is a treasure trove of history.

I'm nearly overwhelmed with the possibilities of what could come next. *Figuring out the mystery clock principle. Getting them all running. Soliciting a museum.*

As the conversation continues, I consciously set the 'next step' thoughts aside and allow my brain to relax. Most important now is to be present for this moment, with these gracious people, at this wonderful milestone.

152

'You make Ripley a "chump."'

—Hugh D. Mabie, shop visitor

CHAPTER 32

September 2022

After only three hours of chit chat and bubble wrap, we have bid our new stepcousins goodbye and pointed ourselves east. The car is packed solid with luggage, travel coolers—and clocks.

Judy Montana has prepared a snack basket for the road, which includes crackers, cheeses, assorted meats and veggies, and cookies.

"She's truly an Allison," I tell my sister, as I assemble a miniature cracker/cheese/tomato sandwich. She grabs a cookie and nods.

The next two days are a mad mix of driving, working, and texting with Judy Montana. My work proposal gets so busy, I end up dropping my sister at O'Hare and diverting to a friend's house in the suburbs of Chicago. I spend the next two days in their basement, head down, working the proposal response, which we finally submit at 11 p.m. that second night.

Driving home the next day is surprisingly emotional for me. After a whirlwind couple of weeks, it's finally just me alone in the car with the clocks and my musings. I queue up the song *Won't Give In* and turn on my phone's video recorder. Something deep is fighting its way out of me; it feels important to capture the moment.

My thoughts fire at will as the song's haunting melody envelops me.

Charley's death.
My dad's death.
My sister Molly's recent death.
My car, full of clocks.

Tears stream down my face. *Grandpa, I didn't give in. I'm carrying it on.*

Pulling into my driveway that evening, I take special care to unpack the car, carrying all the clocks to my office on the second floor. They're still secured in bubble wrap, but I take each step with precision. I greet my husband from a social distance and prepare for my five-day, post-trip quarantine in the guestroom.

Over the next few days, I spend my off-work hours unpacking and photographing each clock. I carry a butcher block table up from my basement storage and spend some time arranging the collection for an attractive-yet-stable display. A couple of gray Rochester afternoons deliver the natural lighting I love for pictures.

I poke through the box of records that Judy Montana provided. There are lots of photos, including some young pictures of my dad that I've never seen before. *He looks like me!* Inside my gut, shock wrestles with something more primal. Not quite pride. Not quite pleasure. Just…connection.

There are papers as well. Charley's passport application. Margie and Charley's marriage certificate. A 'letter to the editor' about watch repair that Charley wrote to a newspaper. I lay each on my scanner and capture electronic copies. As a group, they round out the timeline of my grandfather's life.

With a weekend of quarantine before me, I decide to pick up a project I'd started two years earlier. I'd previously digitized each page of the Allison Watchmaker's guest book, but I'd always wanted to type each signature/comment into a computerized list for easy reading and sorting. *No time like the present.*

Opening a new spreadsheet, I create columns for guest name, guest address, occupation, comment. Now it's just a massive typing assignment—the shop book is 140 pages long.

I put on some energetic music and get to work. I'm only two pages in when I realize that interpreting each shop visitor's individual handwriting is going to be a significant hurdle. For the really tough ones, I expand the scanned pages on my big computer monitor, doing the best I can.

Reading every single entry is something I've never done. The first thing that surprises me is the breadth of people and occupations that visited the shop and appreciated Charley's work. Soldiers, engineers, actors, jewelers, musicians, nurses—all seem fascinated with my grandfather's craft.

> *I stand amazed and speechless before your wonders.*
> *I believe you can make time stand still and repeat itself.*
> *Marvels of the ages…and they say America has only commercialism.*

Two hours later, I've only made it through twenty-five pages. *This is going to take days.* I call it quits for the night, with a vow to return the next morning.

The hours I spend with the signatures over the weekend provide insight into Charley as a person. From his sister Blanche (*He's a crazy guy, but I love him.*) From a woman named Dana Dewberry (*To my best and trusted friend of 15 years acquaintance and still the same old Charley.*) From a guy named Inius Fountaine (*A wonderfully inspiring way in which to start a new year—not only to see Mr. Allison's clocks, which are miracles, but to know and talk to a man who has found himself, and complete happiness and fulfillment, in his work.*)

I notice some people devote an entire page to their own signature. My gut tells me these are probably celebrities—but some names I don't recognize. A comment from a guy named Sterling Holloway (*For "The Wizard of Time" Allison. The Modern Joshua.*) fills Page 90. A quick Internet search pulls up his photo and bio. *Oh that guy!* The voice of animated Winnie the Pooh.

I keep a browser window open on a separate screen and enjoy a bit of 'celebrity chasing' as I work, mining the signatures to discover once-well-known people who visited my grandfather and commented on his craft.

I learn that Gene Krupa (*I'd like to be able to keep time as well as your clocks and watches do!*) was a drummer for Benny Goodman and others. I find out that George Dolenz (*I have met a great artist in meeting you, Mr. Allison.*) is dad to Mickey Dolenz of The Monkees fame. I spend several anxious minutes researching Jack Kennedy's signature on Wikipedia, ultimately deciding that the guy who visited Allison Watchmakers in 1941 (*My respects to a genius…*) was not a young JFK, but most likely a film actor from the thirties.

It takes five days to complete the task. In total, I record 771 signatories, 463 of which chose to leave a comment. I sit back and swivel my neck, working out the kinks. My eyes fall on the butcher block table.

Having the clocks right here with me and having read the shop book in detail, I feel immersed in the 1940s. The voices have spoken directly to me, conversationally, sharing their one-sided dialogue with Charley.

As I shut down my laptop and turn off my desk lamp, thoughts of my grandfather are very close.

'This book is surrounded by the finest time pieces
originated by one of the finest mechanics.'

—*C. Ray Biggs, shop visitor*

CHAPTER 33

September 2022

The next evening, I'm still living in the perspective of a bystander at my grandfather's shop, watching people come and go. So many of the visitors have marveled at the Allison Mystery Clock, I start to feel that scab tugged back once again.

At least I have the small mystery clock. The underlying mechanism is the same.

I pull up the scan I have of the fuzzy 1940s newspaper article from Uncle Gordon about the Mystery Clock. Now that I've digested the shop book, I can look at it with fresh eyes. Besides, it's been a while since I've read it.

Perhaps the most spectacular thing in the shop is what Charley calls his "Mystery Clock." And mysterious it is…

I smile and scroll down.

…The hands are of wood and revolved separately. Taking a yard stick, Charley set the hands spinning at a good speed. When again they assumed the sensible position, they had gained the minute or two that apparently was lost in the spinning.
He has a portable clock actuated by a different principle.

I stop. *DIFFERENT PRINCIPLE!* I hadn't remembered that. My dad told me 'same principle.' But that's just a memory I have from 1981. Here's something in black and white, contradicting what I'd heard. With one sentence, the potential to learn the secret of the large mystery clock from the smaller clock has dissolved.

We need the big mystery clock. I wonder if there's a photo of it in the box?

I dig through the pictures I received from my stepcousin. We turned through them quickly at her house—I haven't had much chance to look at them since I got home. There's more than a hundred black-and-white pictures with curled edges. I sit on the guest bed in my office and examine each, one by one.

Pictures of Charley and my grandmother next to an old-style automobile.

Pictures of the shop in Woodland Hills. Pictures of Charley and Margie at a cabin.

I slow my pace when I hit these. I flip slowly, hoping. *There!* On an interior wall of the shop, a round clock hangs. The photo is too small for me to see details. I lay it on my scanner and soon have a digital replica of this picture to blow up big.

The hands resemble a pair of scissors. They are suspended from a rod hanging down from the number twelve. *This is it!*

I immediately start a new email to Montana.

Hi Judy!

I'm writing because I uncovered something this weekend that has made me a little more sad about the missing "Mystery Clock." When I reread the newspaper article about it--it states that the smaller version is based "on a different principle than the big version." My father had told me that the small version was the same principle as the big version.

So--I don't know which is true. But after reading more than 400 comments from the Shop Book, I'm recognizing that the Mystery Clock was something really special. And now it's starting to feel like a bigger gap in my quest than I originally thought.

I close by asking her to make a last-ditch effort to find the missing clock and I attach the photo. Will she read my email soon? I follow up with a text to let her know an email awaits. Within ten minutes, she texts me back.

I read your email. I'm sad about the clock too.
I sent the photo of what we are assuming is the
mystery clock to my relatives. There's a whole
new family in the house. Everything that was
in there is gone with the exception of a few garage items.
But if that clock was there or is there my cousin would know.
So fingers crossed.

Hope sparks inside my heart.

That sounds good—thanks! If nothing turns up,
I'll consider making a video to continue that small part of the quest.
But I won't let it inhibit the excitement of what we've discovered.

She replies within minutes.

So I just heard back from my cousin.
The people in the house now agree
they've never seen that clock.

The spark flickers out. I type back.

Got it. I guess our best hope is that the smaller version
(the clock with the eagle) will at least be similar in design
and that Mahlon will be able to figure it out. But no guarantees.

It's nearly eleven o'clock and I'm worn out—the ups and downs of the past week have caught up with me. As I prep for bed, my phone buzzes once more.

You know, there's nothing like it when I search online.
It really is a mystery. I can't wait until Mahlon takes
that one apart. Sorry to bug you so late by the way,
I was just ruminating. Have a great night.

No worries. I normally go to bed early and turn my phone off.
But I'm all 'wound up' with Charley stuff tonight. Night.

Me too. Goodnight.

I shut my phone down and crawl into bed. The ball is now in Mahlon's court. I need his help to dissect the clocks. They are the keys to my grandfather's kingdom.

I'll write him first thing in the morning.

'Perfection in an ideal hobby is one of the finest things in life, Charley.'
—*Ruth Smith, shop visitor*

CHAPTER 34

September 2022

I generally remember the route to Mahlon's workshop, but it's been nearly three years, since before Covid, when I last visited. To avoid any missteps, I plug his address into my map app.

I've written him a couple of weeks ago, letting him know my exciting news. He's written back, sharing my enthusiasm, saying 'I don't know what to say other than Praise the Lord!'

This late September Saturday is warmer than usual—which is fine with me. I navigate the highway, then the back roads to my destination. I've brought two clocks just in case—I'm not sure how fast this will go.

The sky is a deep, peaceful blue—*cerulean*, I decide—with wisps of clouds forming random shapes overhead. Tall stalks of corn line both sides of the highway. In less than a month, the trees covering the hilly countryside will be a patchwork of orange and yellow. Western New York in autumn is an artist's dreamland.

Mahlon answers the shop door apologizing. "I wasn't sure what time you'd come," he says. "I've been in the machine shop; my hands are dirty."

"Go do what you need to do," I say to my Amish friend. Nothing can bring me down today—we're getting our first look inside Charley's recovered collection. "You want me to wait up in the workshop?"

"It's as messy as ever."

"Sounds good to me."

Mahlon disappears to clean up. I ascend the two half-staircases to the inner sanctum—the workshop on the third floor. As promised, the main table is littered with letters, tools, and assorted watch parts. There are several Lemonhead hard candies scattered among the tools. I like that Amish doesn't equate to austere.

I take a selfie then settle in my regular spot—a short, round, rolling stool in front of the workbench. A horse neighs somewhere outside the open window. The white cloth that covers the overhead skylight flutters lazily.

159

Mahlon appears and we both smile. I speak first. "Did you ever think I'd be here with more clocks from Charley's collection?"

"I wasn't holding my breath."

I pull back the bubble wrap and, with years of searching now in the rear-view mirror, we begin to work our way through the Allison Timepiece collection.

PART THREE
CLOCKS

THE ALLISON COLLECTION
(in chronological order of examination by Mahlon Shetler)

The BRASS TORSION PENDULUM CLOCK, circa 1948

Opening the cooler, I pull out the first clock I've brought, a glass-encased construction with a round brass weight swinging freely at the base.

Let the disassembly begin!

"It's a torsion pendulum clock," Mahlon explains. He unscrews the casing and peers down into the guts. "They're also called 'anniversary clocks' because they run for over a year. But there's an extra wheel in this one. Probably for longevity. Your grandfather was definitely out to prove he could do things nobody else could. He must have had a very sophisticated machine shop."

By the late 1940s, Charley was making most of the
internal clock parts himself, including his own screws.

"I found some writing on the back of a photo of this one. It says it will run for two years."

Mahlon nods. "I would believe it." He continues to take components apart. His rust-colored shirt sleeves are rolled up to the elbows. "This is different than any other torsion clock I've seen. It's highly jeweled."

He kneels on the floor to get a table-level view of the works. "This is the first double-mainspring torsion clock I've ever seen." He keeps staring. His enthusiasm fills the workshop. "Yup, double-barreled. Never heard the likes, but why not? Why not indeed. This is the nicest torsion clock I've ever seen."

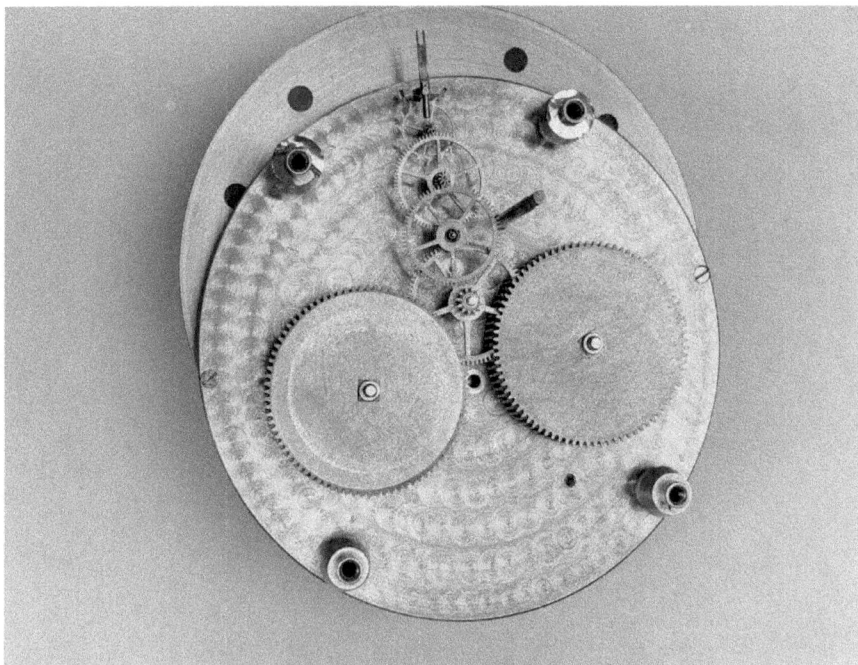

The interior works include two barrels for added power.

Mahlon dives into 'watchspeak.' I furiously take notes. "I am very impressed because this is a very unique situation. It has the quality of an Atmos clock, with features of a hand-wound movement."

"Meaning what?"

"Meaning it has very fine gears." He returns to the stool. "It has a pallet fork like a watch. It's geared way way down. It has a second hand. But it's not a second hand?"

He fiddles with his screwdriver in the back and the second hand spins counterclockwise. "I could just about grin. This is so crazy. There's no way to give a torsion clock a second hand. So he gives it this," he says, pointing to a small dial at the top of the face.

The "second hand" beneath the number twelve.
It rotates counterclockwise and moves one click every six seconds.

He returns to his stool. Mahlon looks briefly at me. "Do you have any pictures of him in his workshop? I'd love to see what type of setup he had."

I shrug. "I'll look."

"It has high quality workmanship throughout. Notice the extensive pearling."

"What's 'pearling'?"

He points to the swirl patterns on the brass components. "That's pearling."

"What's purpose does it serve?"

He smiles. "It just looks nice."

With Mahlon, I feel comfortable asking questions about things I don't understand. His answers never carry judgment. "What does that hanging brass 'cylinder' do?"

Mahlon's not just a watchmaker, he's a teacher. He swivels back and forth on his stool to demonstrate. "It's the pendulum. It rotates back and forth and drives the train. I'll show you once we're done."

The brass pendulum with extensive pearling…just because it's pretty.

Mahlon continues to review the parts—some still attached, some spread out on the bench in front of us. "I'm pretty sure he made his own escapements." He reassembles the clock and hangs the round 'pendulum' on a thin wire. It begins to rotate slowly back and forth.

"Get a picture of this knurling," he directs me, like he always does whenever he sees something noteworthy.

"What's knurling?"

He points to the bumpy surface on the knobs on the top and the back of the clock. I snap a couple of photos with my phone.

167

Charley knurled (added pointy bumps to) several knobs, making them easier to grip.

"Now we need to set the beat."

"And that is?"

"The beat keeps time." He hooks a small electronic device with mini-jumper cables to a couple of spots inside the clock. He sets something inside in motion and the device begins to chirp at regular intervals. "Double tick both ways. It has a very strong beat." He laughs. "This clock is going to run."

Mahlon sticks a screwdriver through a slotted knob at the top of the works. "Take a picture of this. Your grandfather could teach the Germans a thing or two."

I snap a photo with my phone. "What special about it?"

"The Germans designed torsion pendulum clocks—and, in order to set the beat, they actually created a special tool with a long handle to grab this knob and make very fine adjustments. They made it very complicated." He points to the screwdriver. "But Charley simply put a couple of holes through the knob. You can easily adjust the beat with any screwdriver. People in Germany should have thought of that."

The slotted beat adjustment knob allows for easy setting.

He points to the top of the face. "Look at how the second hand works. It records time like a chronograph."

I smile, even though I don't know what a chronograph is. Mahlon's excitement is enough.

"It's a little odd that he used plastic, Lucite, for some of the parts." He stops and thinks. "But it was probably state of the art material at the time."

He moves the clock to a solid table across from the workbench and sets the pendulum spinning. "These clocks are very hard to keep running. They need a very stable base."

We both look at the pendulum as it rotates. With its mini brass barrels and pearling, it's a bit mesmerizing.

Mahlon stands in front of it. "This clock has similarities," he says with his equally authoritative and humble tone, "but no equal that I'm aware of."

The WORLD CLOCK, circa 1952

"This is caaa-razy," Mahlon says, as he stares at the small brass clock. "Your grandfather was absolutely a genius."

I'm learning that my Amish friend seems as excited about finding Charley's collection as I am. "This is really, really nice." He pulls out the photo I sent him a few weeks earlier. "From the picture, I thought this clock was going to be about ten inches tall" (it's actually five inches tall).

He begins the disassembly process. I take notes and snap pictures. As always, we chat. "Every single one is jeweled!" he says. "I have got to do this."

"Do what?"

"I've got to make one."

The World Clock, headless.

The top dial, in two parts.

He carefully pries the circular clock face apart. "It would seem he went the hard way."

"What do you mean?"

He points to the gears. There are many. "Instead of a single gear running all twelve clocks, each one has its own gear."

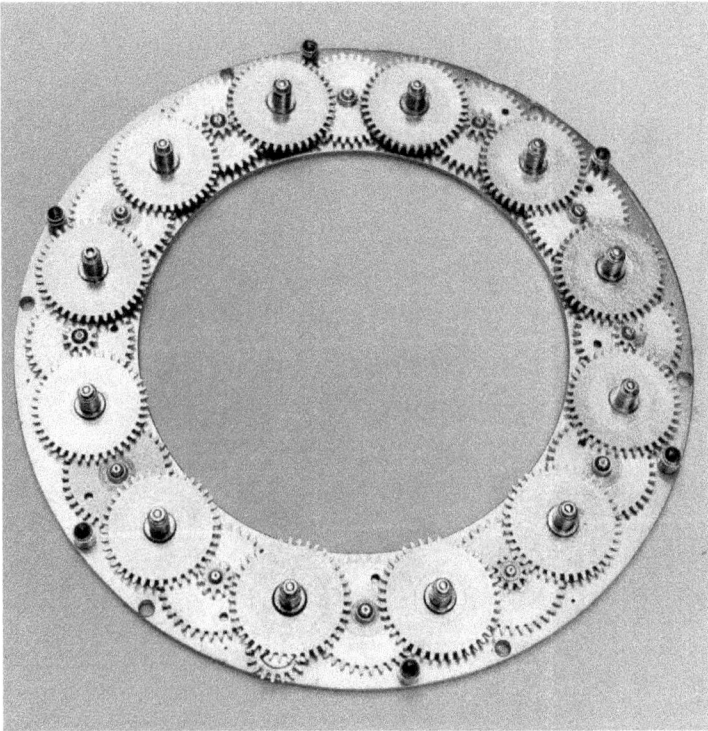

The many gears of the World Clock—
presumably enabling an 'open center' aesthetic.

He pauses, staring at the many parts. "We're gonna do this right."

I raise an eyebrow. "Meaning?"

"I'm gonna take it apart. It's nuts. I think we can handle it."

A fly buzzes by. Mahlon claps his hands together around it and the fly falls to the floor, dead. "They are distracting," he says. "I try to keep flies out of here as much as possible."

I glance at the overhead skylights, covered with a white sheet. There are many, many flies in the warm area between glass and cloth. "It must be a losing battle."

He laughs and points at the front wall of the workshop. "At least I'm glad I put the screens in earlier today." I glance to my left. There are two large windows facing the street. I count at least a dozen flies on the outside of the screens.

"I'm glad too!"

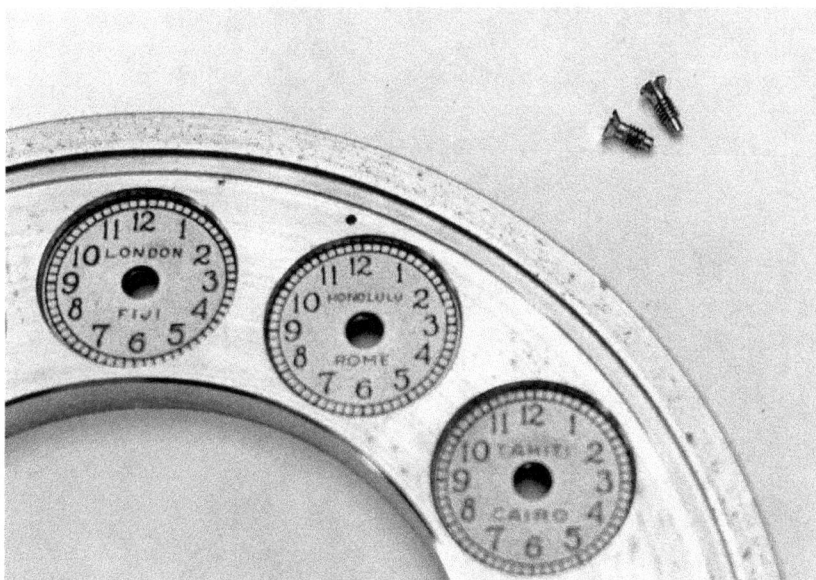

Homemade screws are prolific in my grandfather's collection.

He begins to unscrew tiny screws. "This one has equals...but not this small."

I've noticed that Mahlon's hands tend to shake a little as the day wears on. Yet, when he concentrates on a specific watch task, they are steely.

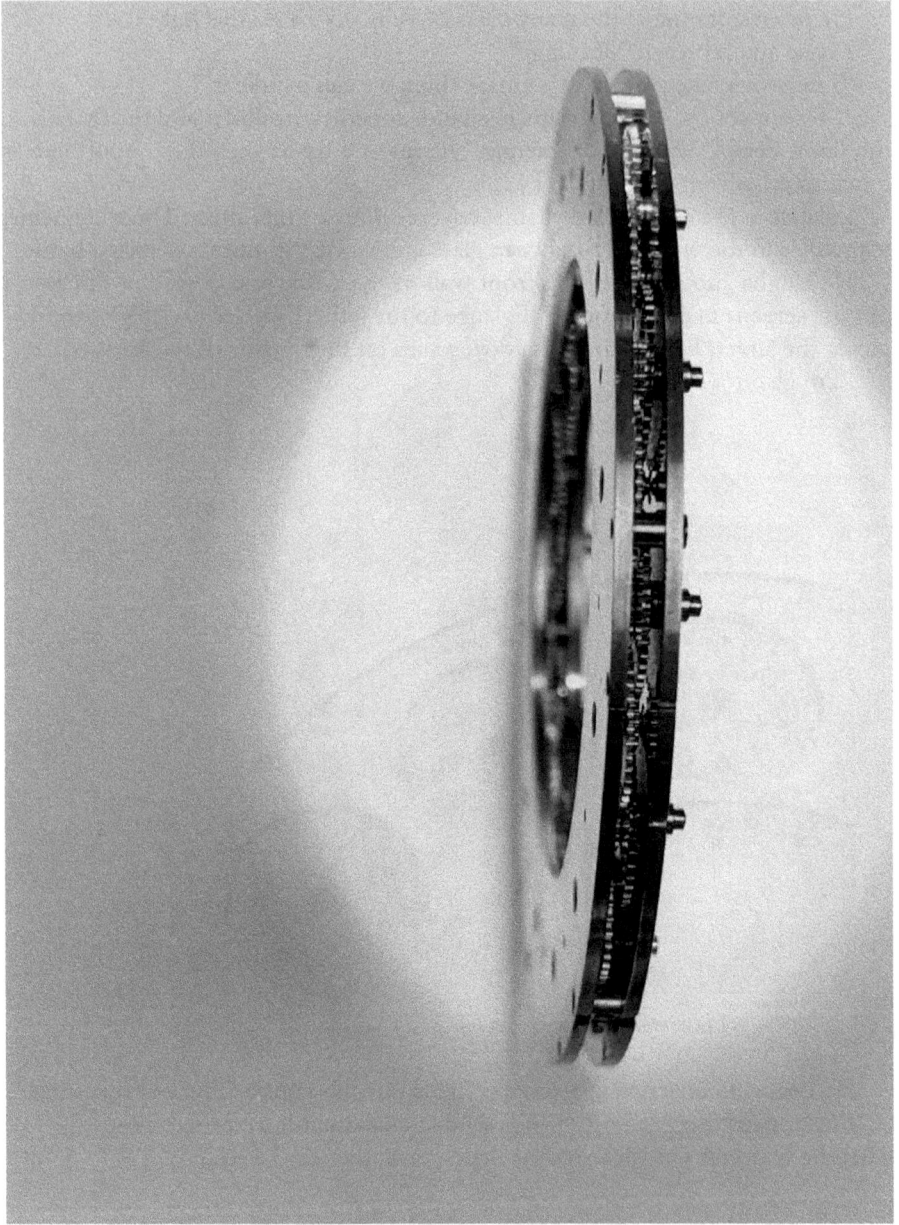

The many-geared clock head, from the top.

He gently pries more of the works apart. His eyes twinkle. "I've never seen anything as jeweled up as this." A fly circles the work area. Mahlon reaches out with one hand and grabs at the air. He gets it!

"I've never seen anybody catch a fly with their bare hands before."

Mahlon laughs and discards the dead fly into the waste basket.

He uses tweezers to lift the hands off each of the twelve tiny dials. "I think these hands are not Swiss made. I think they are American, Charley Allison made."

He sets the parts out on the workbench and gestures for me to take photos. "If you display these in a museum, you'll want to have some quality photos to display, right next to them, so people can see the uniqueness."

Each clock face bears two city names on opposite sides of the world.

"You don't need many photos of the base," he says as he begins to lubricate and reassemble the parts. "It's pretty straightforward. That said, I am enamored with this clock! I have to make one."

I snap a photo or two more. Another fly zooms across the workbench and, again, Mahlon's hand darts out. The buzzing stops.

"Wow!" I say. "You are the fly whisperer!"

I'm never sure if he's going to get my pop culture references, but this one lands well—Mahlon chuckles heartily.

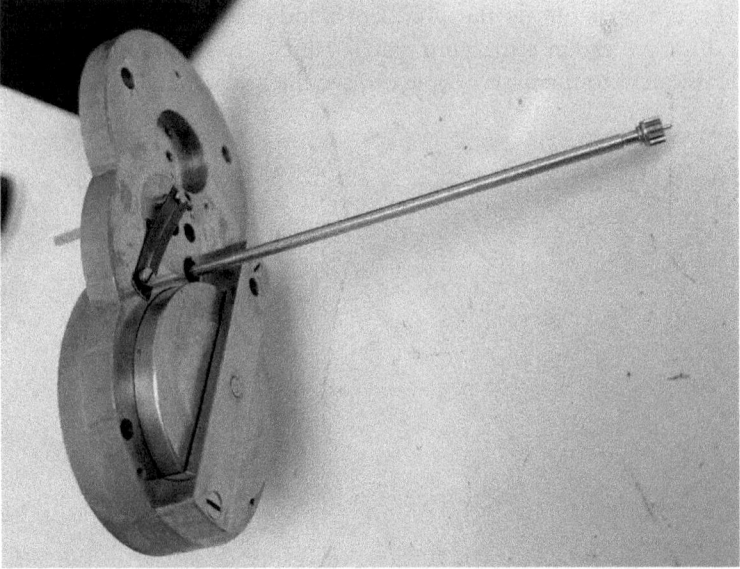

The World Clock with its guts exposed.

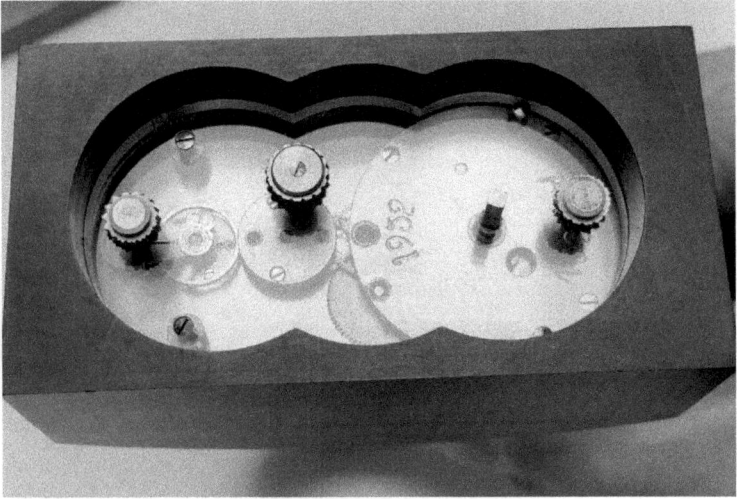

The World Clock view from the base.

The COUPLES CLOCK, circa 1946

"According to what I read on the back of pictures, this one is supposed to be for a couple who sleeps in separate beds, so they can both see the time." I consider adding, "you know, like Lucy and Ricky," but I stop myself. Mahlon *never* gets TV references.

My Amish friend picks up the clock. I can see him enjoying the heft as he examines it. On the bottom, he fiddles with the time-setting mechanism and watches the hands spin in sync. "This is fun!" he says.

Rear view of the Couples Clock.

We dig in. Mahlon removes the glass door on the back of the works, then pauses. He stares at the bottom, removes the screws from the top, and lifts the cover off.

Disassembly of the Couples Clock begins.

We peer inside, our two faces perhaps mirroring the clock's. He pokes around inside. "This clock drives hard," Mahlon says. "It has a lot of torque. I have a feeling this clock will run more than eight days."

Gears branch identically behind each face.

"This clock is more complicated than one would think, for just having two dials," he says.

"Why?"

Mahlon points to the gears. "He made his own cannon pinion. That is really neat. He geared it way down." I'm not sure what all this means...but I take copious notes. I can always look it up later. "It has enough power to drive two dials. And they're big dials!"

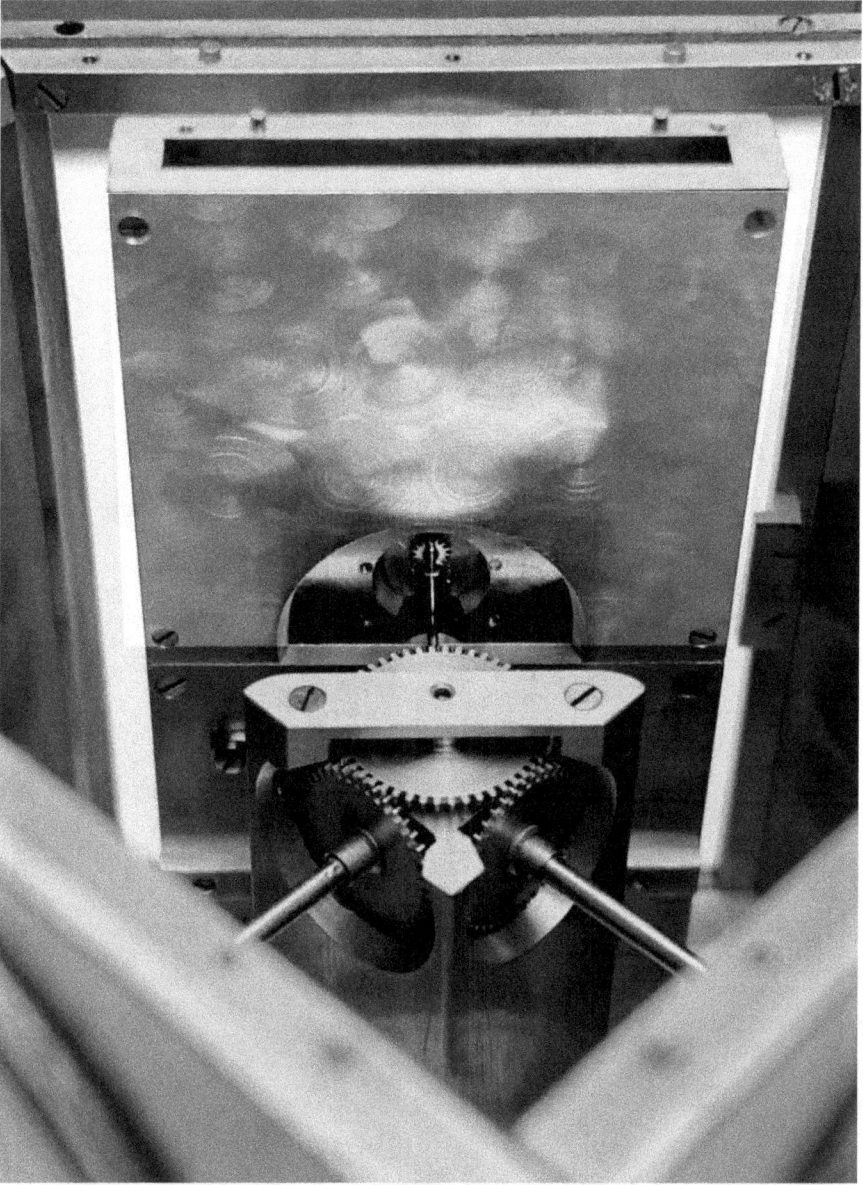

Intricate gearing delivers additional power.

"This collection has such unique properties, it could be written about in a magazine and garner attention. Anywhere they have an appreciation for fine pieces." He smiles at me. "You know what?"

"What?"

"Charley made *timepieces*. They're neither watches nor clocks."

I like the sound of that. More evidence that my grandpa was in a class of his own.

The ART DECO CLOCK, circa 1939

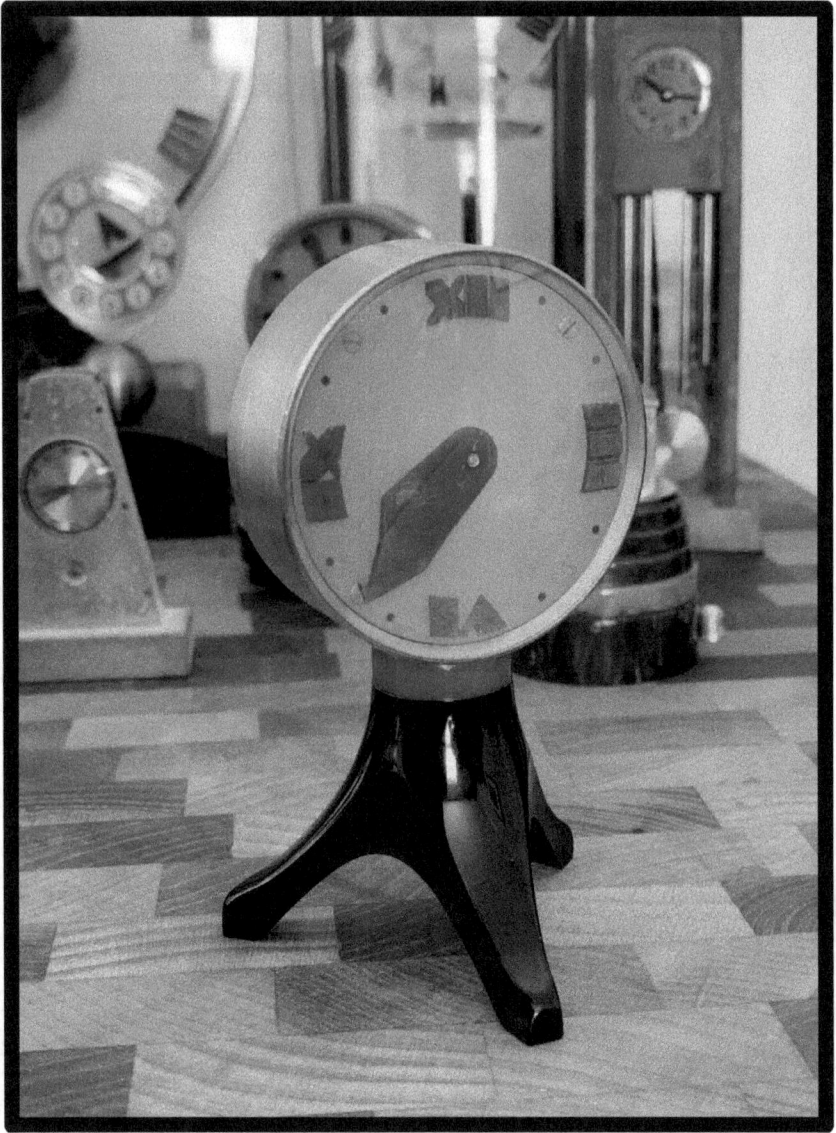

"His simplistic approach is what catches my attention," Mahlon says. "The back glass has beveled indents to allow for the two buttons but still keep all the dust out." He holds the clock out for my inspection. "Not many watchmakers would bother with that."

It's another October Saturday, another date with my Amish friend to dissect my grandfather's clocks. One of today's clocks is a three-legged black-and-gold model. It's not my favorite, but it is interesting to the eye. Its curves and colors remind me of vintage movie theater lobbies.

Mahlon begins taking out screws. "I wonder what we're going to see. I don't think this is just a regular clock. But," he says, looking sideways at me, "it might be."

He pauses and I snap pictures with my phone. We've fallen into this pattern.

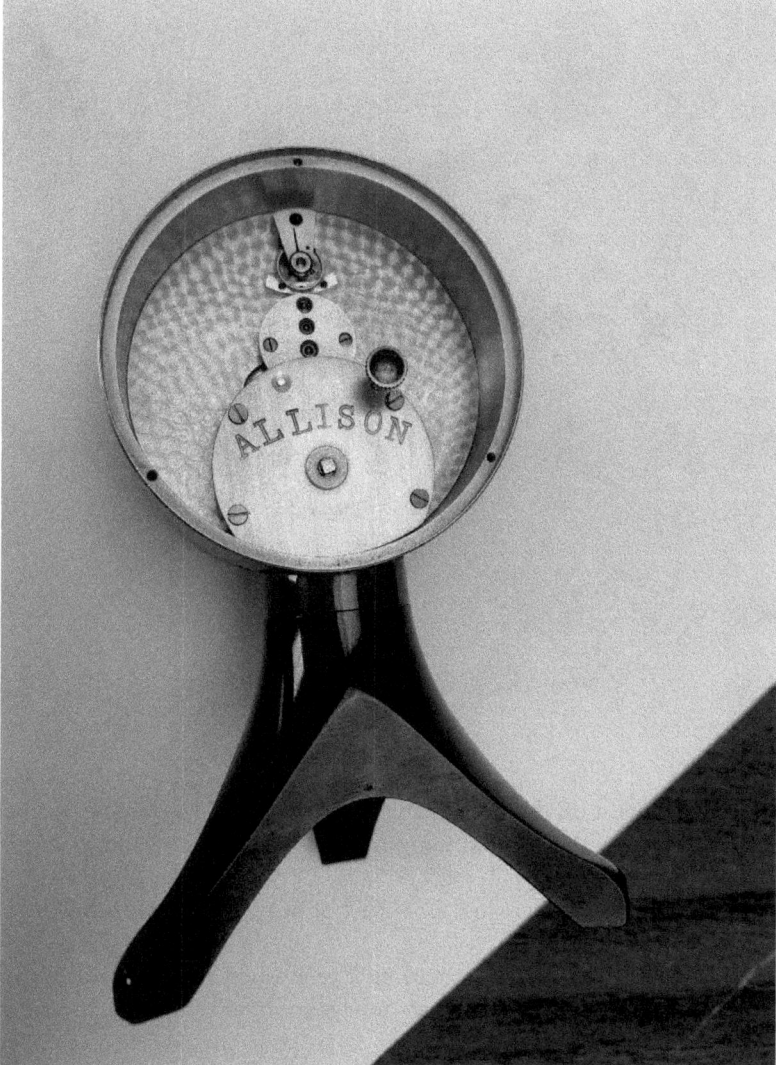

A view of the Art Deco Clock with the back cover removed.

Mahlon squints at the parts as they come apart. "Oh, it does have an extra wheel. It's right there." He points so I can snap another photo.

"What's an extra wheel for?" I ask.

"It makes it run longer. Charley was intent on making long-running timepieces."

Close up of the internal works.

I shift my position on the stool Mahlon has provided. My middle-aged back is not enjoying the lack of lumbar support. But the task at hand overrides my discomfort.

"Honestly, these clocks are just as worthy of being in the Smithsonian as some of the things that are there."

This comment captures my attention! I've learned that, in general, Mahlon doesn't gush about anything—so when he says something like this, it carries extra weight with me.

The mainspring barrel from the bottom view.

He continues the disassembly. "Charley cheated!" he says, raising his eyebrows. "He made a guard pin out of a threaded screw. You don't do that. This may be a first."

He leans in until his loupe goggles are nearly touching the gears. "The pallet fork is a little more crude than the rest of the clocks."

"Why?"

"It was available?" Mahlon shakes his head. "Truly, I don't know." He turns it over, examining the train. "Charley used the latest of the latest lubricant. These all need cleaning…but if they haven't been serviced in seventy years, there's no way they should be running."

The face components are made of Bakelite…a favorite material of Charley's.

I feel a pride swelling within me as I write down his comments. Honestly, it's just watch oil, for heaven's sake, but it feels good. It means my grandfather strived for the best in his craft. And, given what my understated Amish friend is saying, Charley was almost certainly in the top of the ranks.

The components of the Art Deco Clock,
with Charley looking on from the background.

The **PAPERWEIGHT CLOCK**, circa 1938

"Isn't Charley crazy?" Mahlon phrases it more as a statement than a question. I've heard him make similar 'crazy' references about my grandfather's other clocks. He always smiles gleefully when he says it, so I know it's a compliment.

He holds today's clock in two hands. It's a round, plastic-like creation that looks more like a swimming pool float toy than a timepiece. "He wanted to make a clock entirely out of Lucite. So he did."

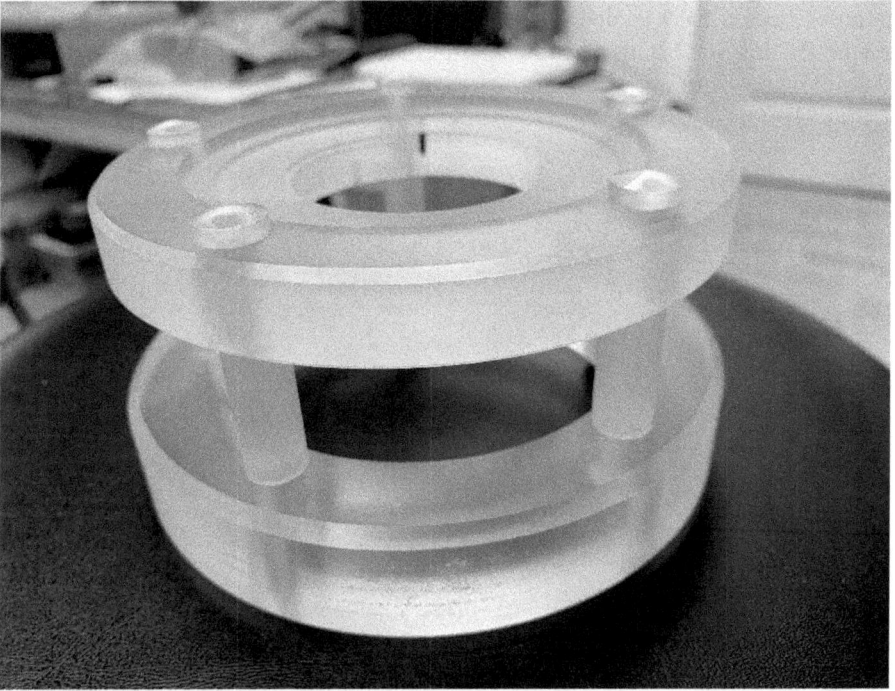

The base, made entirely of Lucite.

Mahlon flips it over and grabs a screwdriver, then laughs. "He made the screws out of Lucite. Now there's a thought."

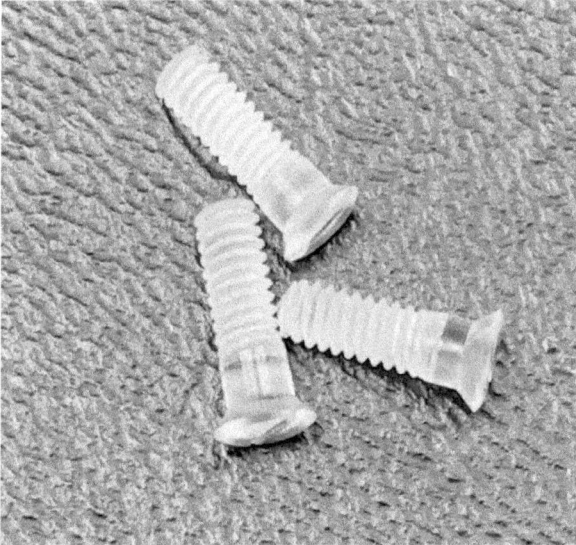

Even the screws are made of Lucite.

I keep a steady eye out for any dates within the works. I've learned that my grandpa occasionally etched the year he made a clock somewhere on the inside plates. As this one begins to come apart, I'm disappointed. It's got the trademark Allison name—but no timestamp.

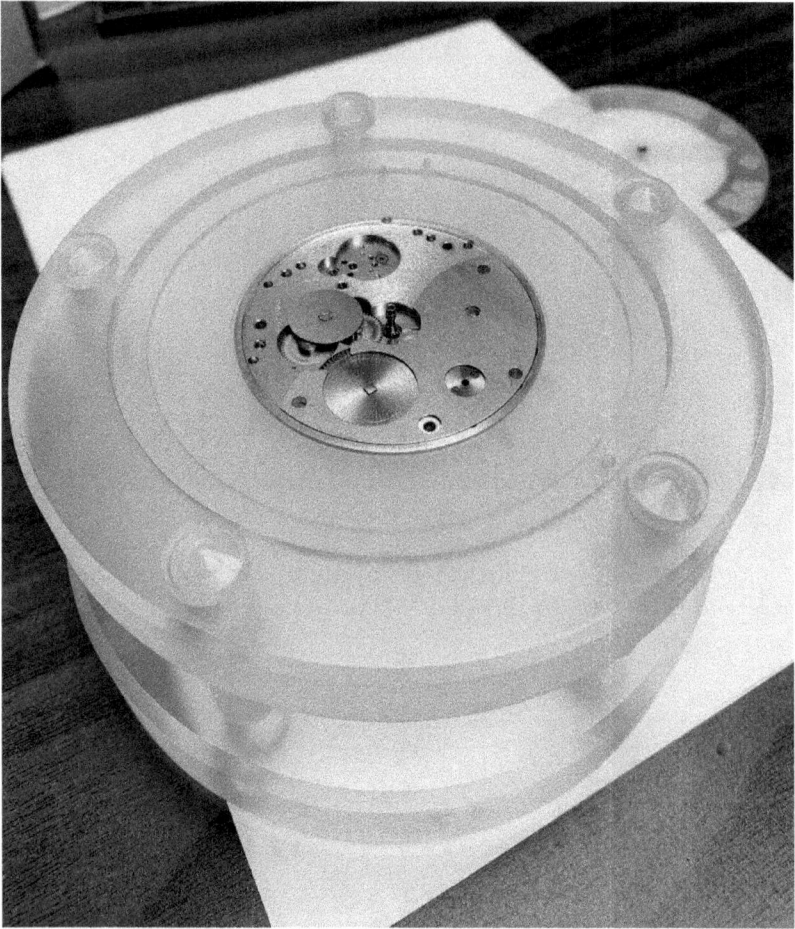

A Waltham car clock drives the Lucite hands.

"There's no date," I state the obvious.

Mahlon's face scrunches as he looks closely at the inner works. "I believe this is one of his earliest. It's a car clock. But he did cheat, the little snicklefritz!"

I laugh. This is not the first 'Pennsylvania Dutch' word Mahlon has snuck into our conversation. "And what does that translate to?"

"Uhh...*mischievous child.*"

"And why is my grandfather a snicklefritz?"

"Because he took the base plate of a Waltham car clock, removed the standard plate, and made his own plate. Then covered it all with Lucite."

Waltham parts on a homemade plate...an early Charley Allison model.

My Amish friend sits back and stares at all the components, set out across his workbench for me to take photos. "I believe this is one of his first pieces."

"And why do you think that?"

"Just based on the complexity of his other clocks." He points to various components. "He took this plate and modified it, put jewels in, but he didn't put some of the finer touches on this one. For example, he didn't pearl the plates in this one," he says.

I look at the smooth surface of the components and nod. This one is clearly not as fancy as some of the others. It's also a little hard to read the white hands on a white face. "It would probably be good on a desk as a paperweight."

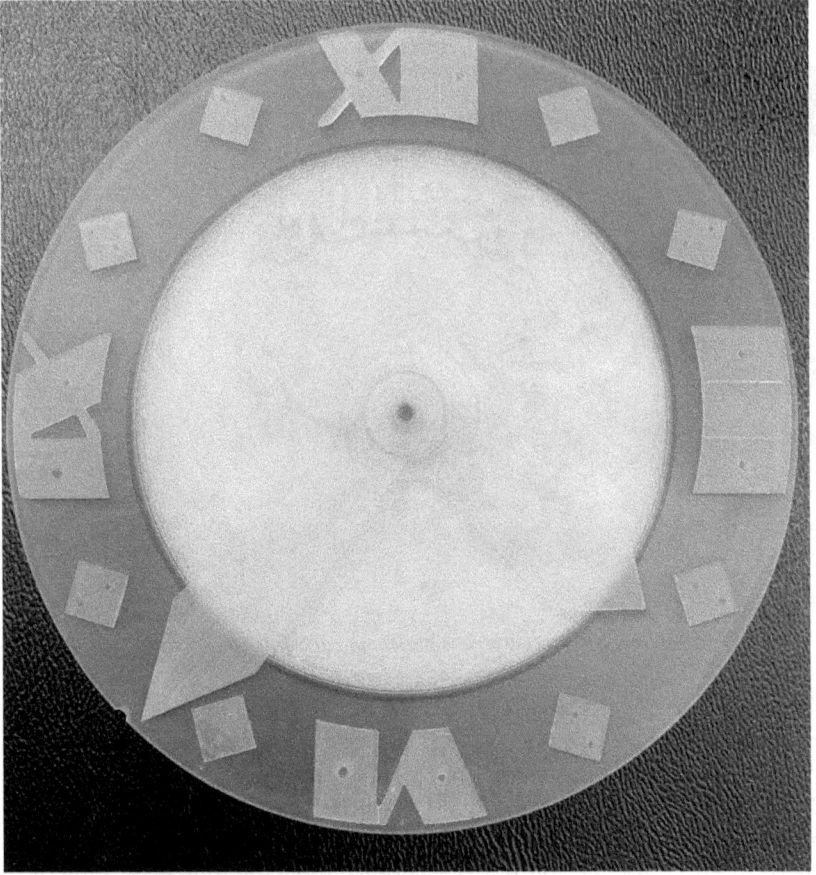

Lucite hands don't offer a lot of contrast on this dial.

The MINI-STEEPLE CLOCK, circa 1937

Here we are, back in Mahlon's workshop, examining the Mini-Steeple Clock. Late October sun streams through the overhead skylights.

He disassembles the steeple, but struggles to remove the plate beneath. "This one is going to be a little different," he says. I stay quiet, giving him space to work his magic.

He pokes, prods, sighs. "We're going to have a bit of an issue." He looks sideways at me. "The barrel won't slide off. It's caused the brass to corrode where it touches the Bakelite."

"What do you recommend?"

"Give me a minute." He gives it one more sturdy pry and off it pops. I smile as we peer into the works.

The steeple's underbelly.

"He bought the materials for this," Mahlon says. "This is another early one. He took a movement and sanded down the name. In later clocks he would have made the case."

Partial disassembly.

He disassembles the entire clock, then stares into the turret section. "This is really sweet."

I like it when Mahlon gets excited about my grandfather's craft. "What's so special about this one?"

He looks like a coal miner as he tips up his goggles and smiles. "Well, it's rather neat, as usual. It's just like a standard turret clock, nothing greatly unique about it. It's just very nicely done."

Four interlocking fittings drive the four faces.

I want to make sure he doesn't miss the worn city names. "Can you see where it said New York on this face?" I point while rotating the steeple. "And Chicago, Denver, Los Angeles?"

"Yup. We could probably clean that up a little. In fact, we'll need to schedule a full day to clean the whole collection."

City names (New York, Chicago, Denver, Los Angeles) are worn, but discernable.

Mahlon examines the rest of the works. "He polished off the identifying marks...maybe so he could put his name on it. But this one is not signed." He chuckles softly. "He was working his way up a ladder. Maybe this is his first piece."

That sounds right to me. Of the entire collection, this is the only clock that has to be wound every day. I nod in agreement and continue to take notes.

The GREENWICH MEAN CLOCK, circa 1940

"This clock has some moments of interest and moments of sloppiness," Mahlon says. "Was Charley maybe under stress when he made this one?"

I think of the timeline I've uncovered of my grandfather's life. 1940 is one year before the tumultuous divorce from Grace. *His third marriage was disintegrating.* "I'm guessing he was," I reply. I find it fascinating that a watchmaker in 2022 can trace the temperament of a watchmaker in 1940, just by examining his work. Mahlon continues.

"He has a new trick to every piece. He used the dot system," he says, pointing to small marks on the twin faces. "These two dots line up with those two dots, and so forth." My Amish friend smiles. "You can't put it together wrong."

I glance at the photo of my grandfather that I've placed on the workbench. This one is of father and child. My dad, maybe four years old, standing at his father's knee. I let my mind drift.

"Wouldn't it be fun to spend an afternoon with Charley?"

Mahlon glances at me as he eases out the tiny screws. "But would we be satisfied with just one?"

I laugh.

"What year was Charley born?" he asks.

"1892."

"He used an 1892 Waltham barrel and balance cock screws. I'm sure it's just a coincidence…but interesting."

Mahlon tries to pull the works out of the base. It doesn't come apart. He examines it closely.

"This seems like early Lucite. It shrank, probably from being in that hot California closet for seventy years. It's holding onto the movement plates."

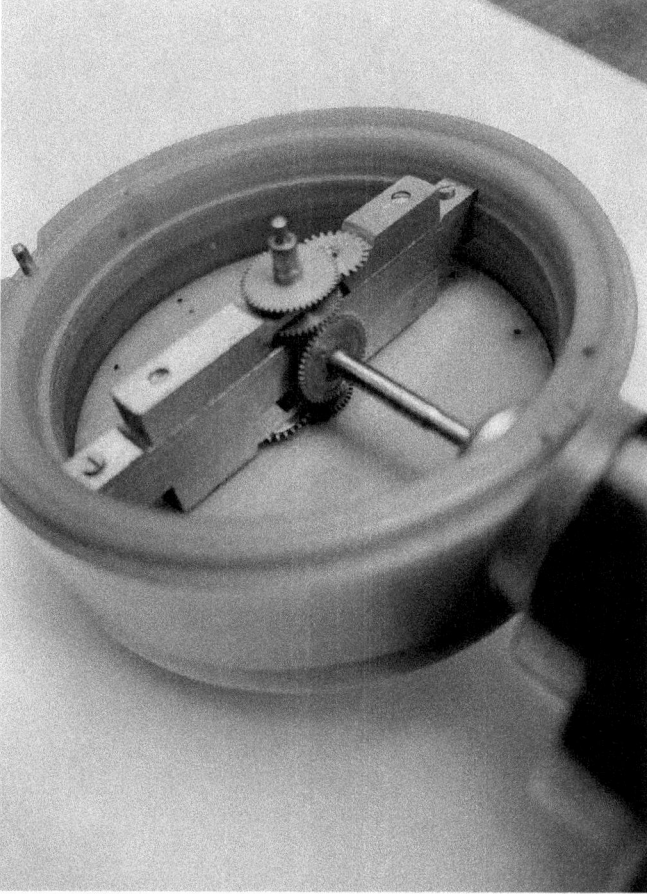

The metal crossbeams have prevented horizontal shrinkage over time…but not vertical.

He retrieves a heavy-duty screwdriver from the piles of tools and watch parts that encircle us. He lays a cloth against the clock housing before continuing. Mahlon has a universal rule that I've learned: Do No Harm.

He positions the screwdriver and slowly applies pressure. Nothing. He sets all the pieces down and sits back on his stool, letting out a long breath.

"We have a problem," he says, staring at the clock. "I can try applying more pressure to the plate—but I risk bending it or, worse, cracking the base." Now he's looking at me. "Or, I can use my lathe to shave a tiny bit of the Lucite off where it has shrunk. Just enough to ease those works out of there. It'll change the clock from its original state a tiny bit—but I just don't see any other options." He's encouraged me from the start to keep everything as Charley originally created it. This would be our first, albeit small, alteration.

1940…a difficult year in my grandfather's life?

I look at him, then pick up the clock, turning it over. I don't want to risk something we can't fix. But I'm anxious for all of the clocks to be in working order. If we can't get it apart, we can't clean it, we can't set the hands, and it probably won't run after seventy years of captivity.

I've learned to trust Mahlon's judgment. "What do you recommend?"

He thinks for a moment. "I'd trim the plastic. But it's your clock, your choice."

I hand it back. "Go for it."

He moves to his lathe on the other side of the room and snaps a few parts into place, including a small cutting tool. He pumps the floor pedal and the lathe begins to spin. "Charley would have had electric," he says over the sound of the machinery. "But this will work just fine."

With careful precision, he brings the blade to the base of the clock, which is now spinning on the lathe. Thin plastic shavings peel off. Mahlon pauses, puts on a mask, and continues. "Sometimes I forget what a mess this can be."

A small pile of black shavings accumulates beneath the spinning clock. "There," he says. "That should do it." He takes off his mask and we return to the regular work bench. "Here goes," he says, applying pressure once again. The movement plate plops out neatly into his hand. Mahlon smiles and sighs at the same time.

"I know you said it's okay if we break something," he says.

It's true, I've tried to help him relax by telling him know it's okay if something breaks on any of these clocks. After all, we're resurrecting machinery after seventy years in a closet. The possibility for casualties is very real.

"But," he finishes the thought, "I'm glad it came out without any damage!"

I laugh with him.

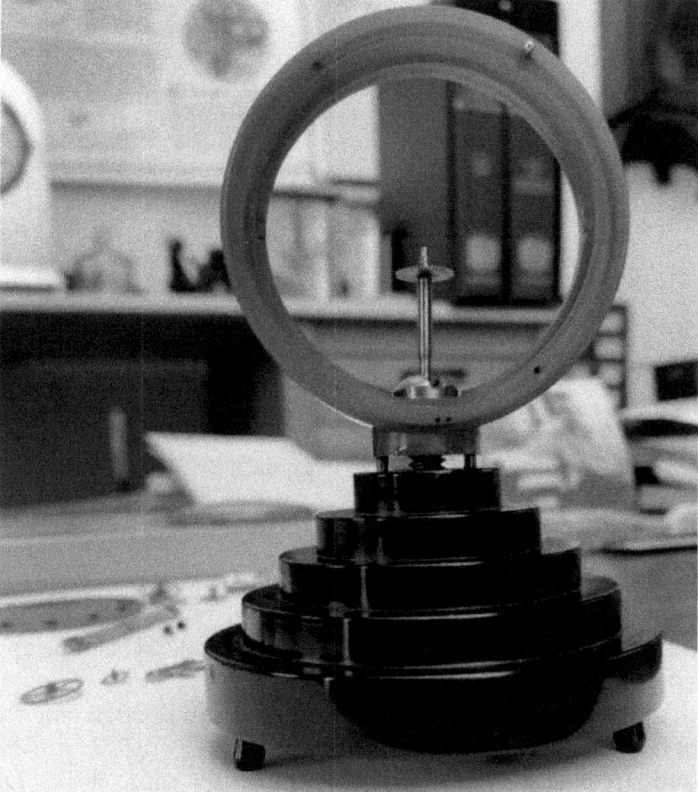

After much coaxing, the clock comes apart.

Within an hour, the clock is completely disassembled and he's done some brief cleaning. He doesn't have the equipment for full cleaning anymore—that's something we've scheduled with a friend of his for a future session. For now, it's a crap shoot whether each clock will run or not.

Many parts of this clock come in identical pairs.

"So we have to set the difference between the faces when we put the hands on, right?"

"Right." He uses tweezers to grab the first hour hand. "What time do you want on each side?"

I check my cell phone's world clock, just to confirm London time. "One side, New York time, the back, five hours later."

His hands are precise as he quickly reassembles the entire clock. "Done." He gives it a full wind and we watch it run for a couple of minutes.

"Nice," he says.

The BAKELITE TORSION PENDULUM CLOCK, circa 1941

"Oh what a sweet clock," Mahlon whispers. It's another Saturday, another Charley clock. The November drive through the southern tier New York has treated me to a late-autumn array of red and gold foliage.

Mahlon makes a general fuss about each Charley clock, so I always dig for specifics.

"Why sweet?"

"What makes it sweet is that it's see-through."

It's interesting to watch all the gears turn.

He begins to tinker. "This is definitely not a 400-day clock."

"Why?"

"Because of all the gears." He points to the brass workings. I nod as if I recognize the uniqueness. But I'm still pretty new to the clock game.

The torsion pendulum has a sliding-weight regulator.

Mahlon continues. "There are two extra jewels than normal in here. My goodness, this thing has power! There's not much we need to do with this one." I smile and write. And smile and write.

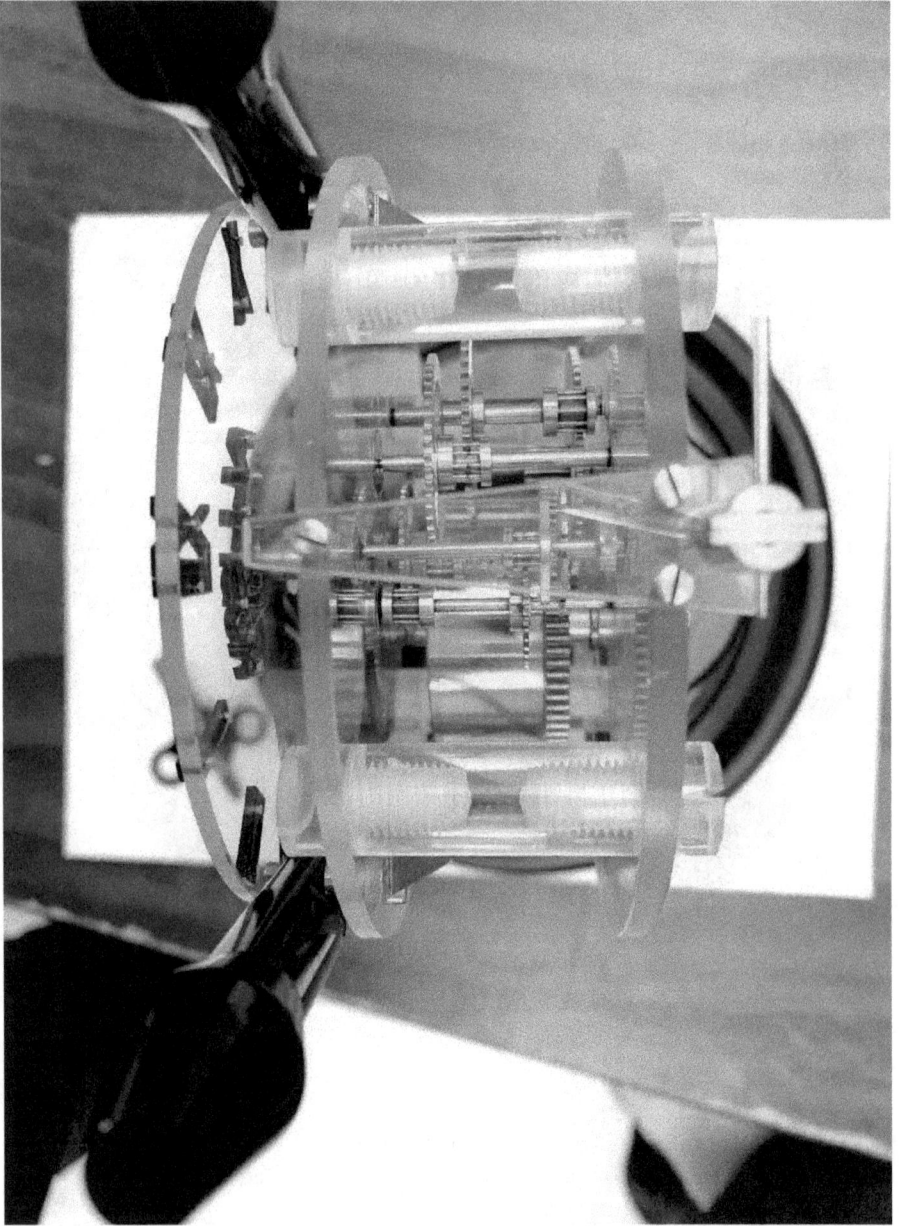

A bird's eye view of the Bakelite Torsion Clock.

The POLE CLOCK, circa 1945

It's the Saturday after Thanksgiving. It's an extraordinarily warm November, so my drive south is another easy excursion. I feel my mind untether against the expansive fields and tree-topped hills.

Mahlon's wife is walking along the driveway. We exchange waves as I lug today's clock into the workshop. It's the heaviest of my grandfather's collection— a transparent circle atop a three-foot metal pole.

As always, Mahlon begins by looking it over. "This is the first clock I've seen with a weight-driven balance escapement." He pulls out his screwdriver and the disassembly begins.

The Pole Clock with the rear cover removed.

"He didn't make all of it...but he made most of it."

"Which parts does he buy?" I ask. In my perfect vision of Charley, I imagine him leaning over his tools, sweat dripping from his brow, crafting each piece by hand. I've learned to accept that beginning with some existing parts still leaves plenty of room for creativity.

"He often started with Waltham watch parts. And he most likely bought the jewels. But, based on the vision of what he wanted to create, he then started making his own plates and screws and gears and whatever he needed to make it work."

The plates form an unusual shape.

"Charley definitely favored Waltham. You should visit the town sometime. It's in Massachusetts."

"Is the Waltham Watch Factory still there?"

Mahlon shakes his head. With no factory, I most likely won't visit. *But maybe they have a museum.* I take a note to add this to a list of possibilities for showing the collection.

"Charley, you are a little bit tricky here." Mahlon points. "There's a screw within a screw. You'll probably want a picture of that."

I snap the shot as Mahlon studies the back cover of the works, a clear circle of Lucite.

A screw within a screw, as shown in the top right of this photo.

"Okay, Mr. Allison, you've got me baffled just a little bit." He stars at it, then holds it out to me. "Charley made a mistake. First one. He did a double-hole drill."

I look at it, then at Mahlon. "I find that hard to believe." I take the cover from him and gesture with it. "Knowing what we know about Charley, if he made such an obvious mistake, don't you think he'd just get a new piece of Lucite and start over?"

He nods in agreement. "Let's keep looking."

"The hands are rosewood," he notes.
"Is that anything special?"
"It's just what he chose. It's nice."

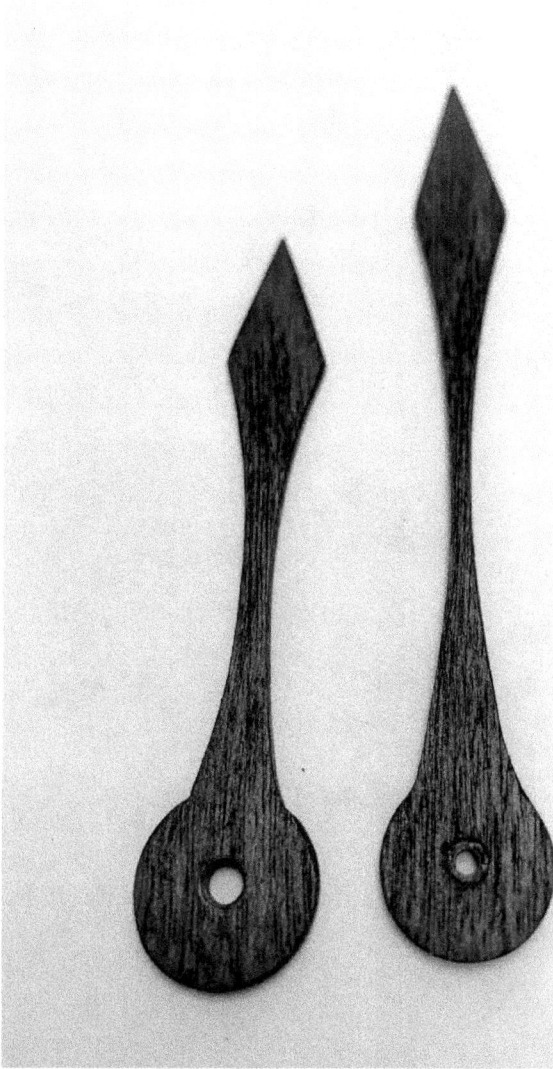

Hand-crafted rosewood minute and hour hands.

Mahlon takes some time looking at the pole itself. "He went to great trouble to make this…and I'm not sure why yet. It involves angles and details that you normally wouldn't have to worry about."

This bracket has unique curves…why?

"It's probably one of his earlier models. I don't see any pearling." He sets all the parts out for me to get a comprehensive photo. "He made the plates. He didn't make the train."

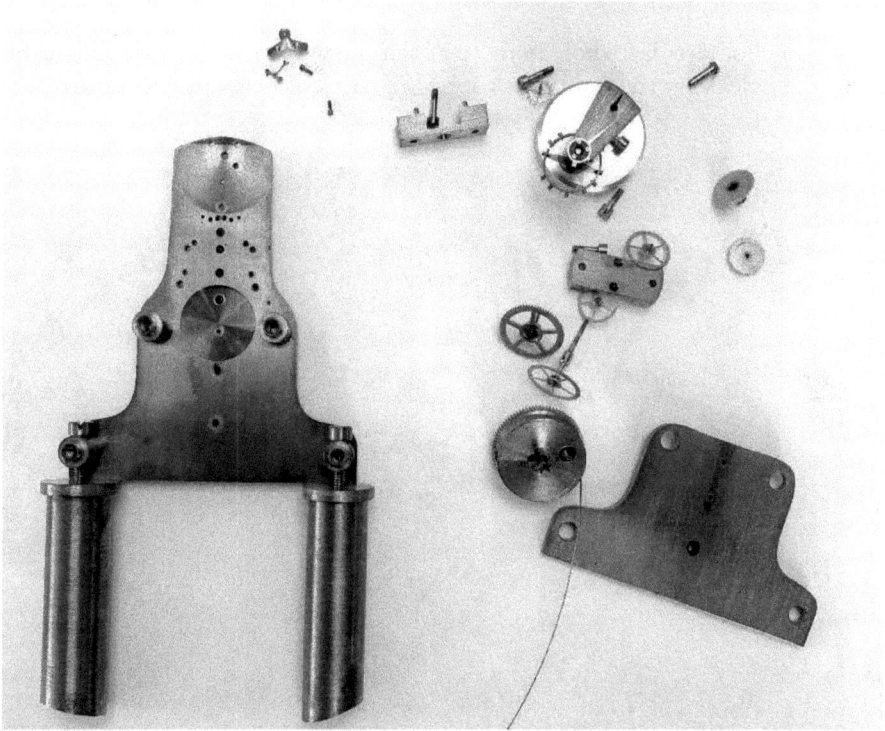

The Pole Clock parts…sans the pole.

"With a little bit of TLC, we can make this run, I think." Mahlon takes a few minutes to lubricate the pallet and mainspring at his other bench. I use the time to snap some additional photos.

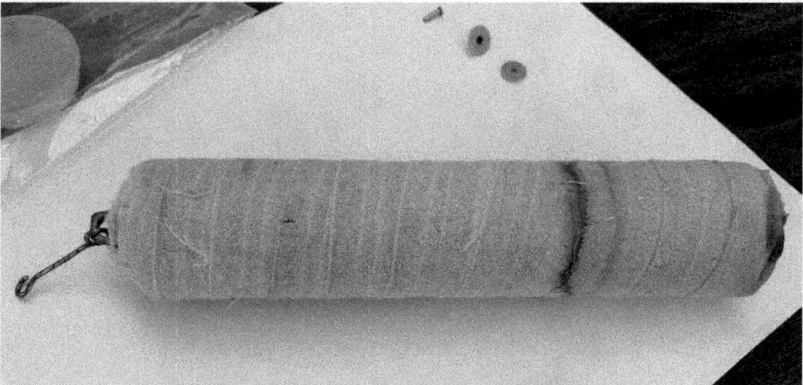

A weight, wrapped in cloth, powers the train from inside the main support pole.

He returns and begins to reassemble the works, then the covers. "I have figured out the double hole!" he says gleefully. "It's to line up the back cover."

I'm relieved that Charley hasn't settled for a mistake. My impression of his fine standard of artistry remains intact.

Mahlon contorts his whole body to attach the weight to its suspension cable inside the pole. Very soon, the clock springs to life...keeping perfect time.

Attaching the weight to the 1/32-inch cable inside the pole is a challenge.

The **ALPHA-OMEGA CLOCK**, circa 1944

It's November and we're looking at the smallest clock in the Allison collection, a two-inch-tall obelisk. The outside casing is made of the same gritty aluminum as the Mini-Grandfather. Mahlon turns it over and studies the back.

"This one has started rusting." He pulls a screwdriver from his ever-present rack of tiny tools and tries to turn one of the six screws holding the back plate on. His face scrunches.

"We gotta be careful." He sets the screwdriver down and begins to dab oil onto each screw. "I think if we can get this back cover off, the rest will slide out."

We chat for a minute, allowing the oil to seep in.

"Why 'Alpha and Omega', Charley?" Mahlon asks.

I shake my head. "I don't think he was very religious."

"Do you know what Alpha and Omega mean?"

"If you mean the Greek letters, sure, the first and the last. I took a year of Greek in high school."

Mahlon smiles, as if I've impressed him. He takes the screwdriver in hand and tries to coax one screw out. It won't budge. "We have to be very careful. If we apply too much pressure, the screw itself will break."

I'm always fighting the struggle of keeping my unskilled hands off the merchandise versus wanting to dive in with my DNA to guide me. Today, I lean into my DNA. "Can I help?"

"Actually yes." He sets the clock on a clean sheet of paper. "If you can hold it in place, I can use two hands to work the screw."

This move doesn't require any skill. I grip the clock as Mahlon firmly twists. One screw begins to give. He oils and turns, oils and turns. After more than a minute of coaxing, the screw finally backs out of its hole.

Mahlon holds it up horizontally. "See the corrosion?" I look closely. There is white crud up and down the screw, like you might see on a battery that has gone bad. "This is gonna be tough."

After resting for a couple of minutes, we try a second screw. This one is less cooperative.

"Okay, we need to try a different approach." He sits back and sighs.

"What if we soak the whole thing in oil for a while?" I offer.

He shakes his head. "It might discolor the dial." He thinks for a minute. "Let's soak this from the outside in. If you can get ahold of a lubricant called Kroil and put a dab on each of these screws every day for a week, we might have some better luck."

I grab my phone. "How do you spell that?"

"K-R-O-I-L."

I do a quick search and find a small can on Amazon for $21. "It'll be at my house in two days."

Mahlon laughs.

It's mid-December and I've already been back to Mahlon's twice. I've been diligently applying the Kroil to the Alpha Omega Clock.

In late November, Mahlon coaxed out two more of the six screws, but the other three wouldn't budge. He sent the clock and me home for more oiling.

Today, I've got my fingers crossed. If the screws don't come out, we might have to do some actual surgery on this clock—altering what my grandfather created. Neither of us want that.

We start the now-familiar procedure. I hold the clock; Mahlon uses one hand to tap on the screwdriver with a mini-hammer and the other hand to turn.

Screw #4 slowly inches its way out. "I think we're gonna make it!" he says.

Screw #5 is actually a little easier. I smile. "One to go!"

As if we were in a movie, Screw #6 won't budge. Nadda. Mahlon taps and turns, taps and turns. It rotates a tiny bit. "C'mon!" I encourage it. He grits his teeth and uses both hands to carefully-but-firmly rotate the screwdriver. It makes one more small rotation, then stops. A few more attempts produce zero movement.

Mahlon breathes out. "Let's take a break for a minute."

We sit back and look at it. "You know," he says, "I don't think we have to get this last one all the way out. It's out far enough I think I can rotate the back cover." He fiddles with it for a minute and the back cover swivels out. Mahlon gently pulls at the works, which slide easily out of the aluminum.

"We did it!" I am all smiles.

A lone holdout—the bottom left screw.

"It's another Waltham piece," he says. Mahlon picks up a toothpick and a small bit of clay. He dabs at each of the components, removing the white gunk where he can. "There's corrosion here I've not seen with other of Charley's pieces."

"It's a wristwatch train, not a pocket watch."

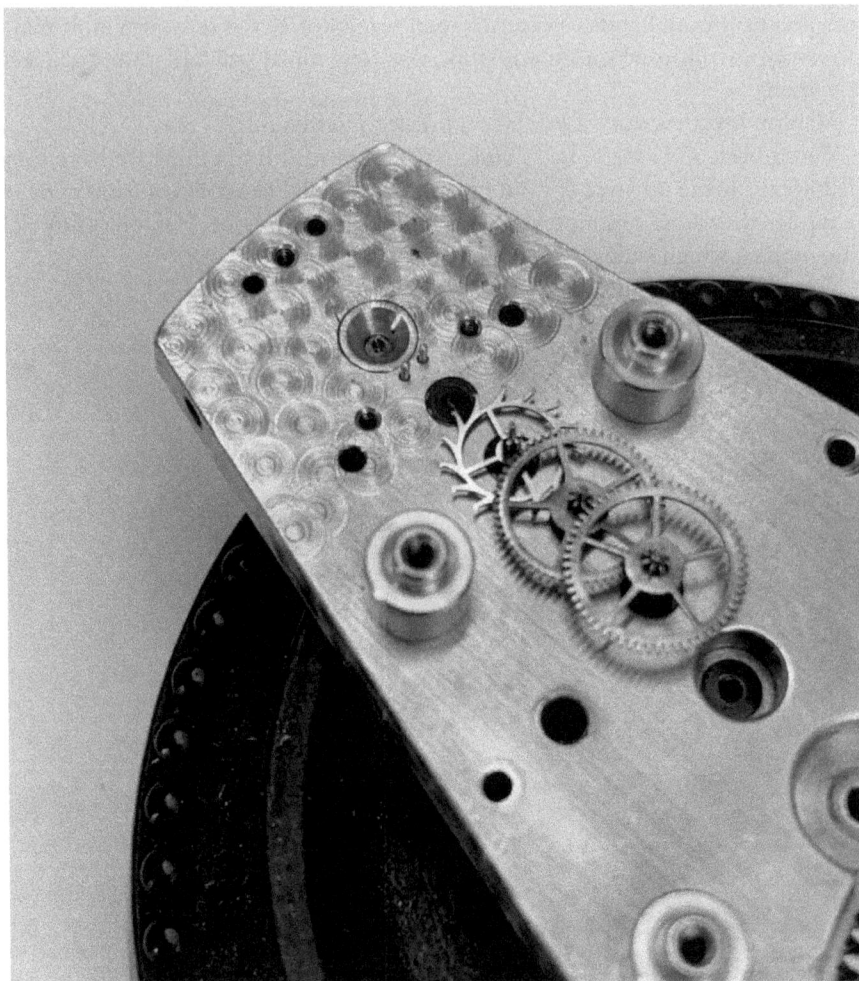

Jewels and gears inside the Alpha Omega Clock.

Once he's cleaned the dirty parts that were in touch with the aluminum outer casing, he begins the job of disassembly. The insides are much cleaner—like the rest of Charley's clocks.

I note the pearling of the inside plates, which is not visible from the outside. More of Charley's 'classy interiors'—for watchmakers' eyes only.

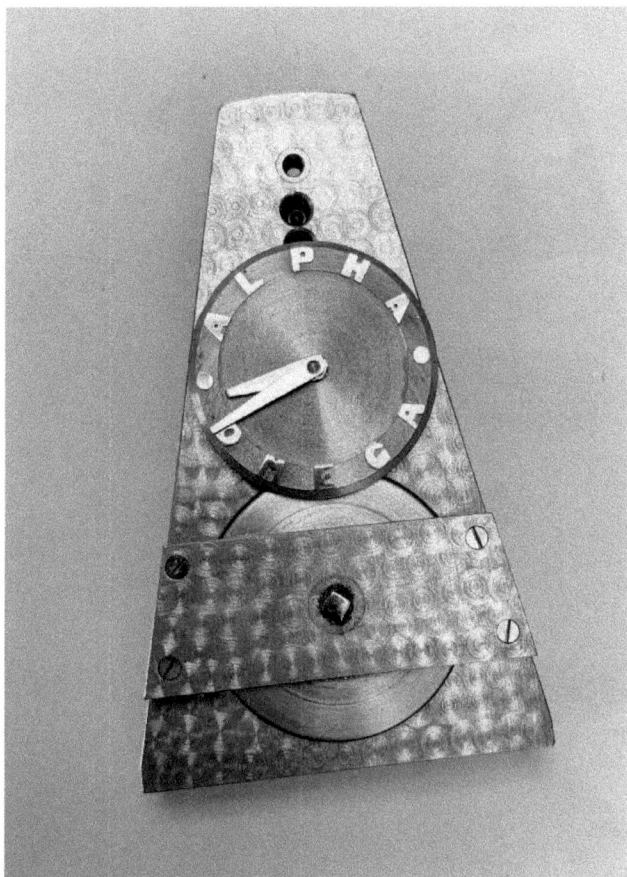

Pearling only a watchmaker will see.

Mahlon begins lubricating the moving parts. We chat—about the lack of snow this season, about the waning daylight, about the Amish genealogy book he is writing.

Dusk is falling when he begins reassembly. With no electric lighting, this is a potential problem. But we've run up against dusk before, so I've come prepared.

Battery-operated lights are allowed, so I've brought a small camping lamp and a couple of clip-on book lights. Mahlon has a flashlight headband. Between the two of us, we generate enough light to put the clock back together.

*Due to aluminum corrosion, the littlest Allison clock
is also the most difficult to disassemble.*

Why Alpha and Omega? I have guesses, but no definitive answer.

Mahlon gives it a full wind and, in the near darkness, we watch it tick along. "I feel like Charley's children are coming back to life," I say.

He chuckles. "This one was really dead."

220

'These clocks are the nearest thing to magic I have ever seen.'
—Effie Hill, shop visitor

CHAPTER 35

December 2022

A light snow has settled over Mahlon's hillside. I pull up next to his workshop and park, making sure to leave clearance for horses coming in or out.

I'm extra excited—we've reviewed eleven of the clocks, saving the best for last. Today we'll dig into the most important Allison creation: the small American Mystery Clock. Today I might learn the secret my grandfather dreamed of. Or…not.

I stand outside my RAV4 and unload clocks, notebook, camper lamp—all the equipment I've found helpful during these sessions. The family hound, a skinny brown-and-white mutt named Penny, tentatively approaches my car. I'm not sure if she's generally shy or simply skittish around motor vehicles, but it's usually a crap shoot whether she'll actually come close. Today she makes it within ten feet, then reverses course.

Mahlon answers my knock and we climb the stairs to his third-floor workshop. I have quite a few things to discuss with him. The set knob has popped off one of the other Allison clocks. The piece he's written about Charley for the NAWCC Bulletin needs review. We take care of other business quickly.

"Let's get to the Mystery Clock!" he says. "I want plenty of time with this one." The anticipation in his tone matches my own. After three years, my Amish friend is as invested in my grandfather's collection as I am.

I unwrap the bubble wrap. "I'm hoping that this little American Mystery Clock will help us figure out how the big Allison Mystery Clock worked."

Mahlon takes it in both hands and squints at the front, then the back, then the sides. "If it's as I think it is, it's ingeniously laid out."

"I'll take pictures like normal," I say, "but I'm not publishing them." I look sideways at him. "If we figure it out, I'd like to ask that we keep Charley's secret between us. I mean I'll tell my family," I continue, "but I don't want to give away the magic."

"Agreed," he says.

An hour later, we've disassembled, photographed, and reassembled the

American Mystery Clock. I've seen its design and, I don't know if it's because I've soaked up some watchmaking in the past three years, *but it actually makes sense to me.*

"Mahlon, *we solved it!!*" I cheer. "This had *got* to be the design he thought of in a dream!"

Mahlon swivels the clock horizontally to get the hands moving, then stands it upright. They rotate for a few spins, each moving independently of the other, then they settle back onto the correct time. "I'll have to do some research on mystery clocks to see if this design is truly unique," he says, chuckling. "But, can you imagine how fascinating this would have been in Charley's shop?"

I nod and pull out the photo of the large Allison Mystery Clock—the one that's still missing. "I guess the little one really was built on a similar principle! You know," I say, "given what we've learned today, I actually think you and I might be able to recreate Charley's big mystery clock. It might not be exactly the same as the little one but, in my mind, I have an idea of how it might work."

I take the clock from the workbench and tip it to get the hands spinning. "I mean, I can't guarantee that it will be exactly the same as Charley's, but I think it would work like the newspaper article describes it."

Mahlon laughs again. "I'll do some research."

To my ears, that's as good as concurrence.

As I rewrap the clock for travel, I'm contemplative. In many ways, today's session has wrapped up the quest I started back in 1981—to solve the mystery of my grandfather's mystery clock.

A question crosses my mind. "So, what do you think Charley would think of you and me, if we all hung out for a week?"

Mahlon smiles at the thought. "I think we'd get along fine," he says.

That night, driving home along the snowy country roads, I think about all of the threads that have intertwined to bring me to where I am. My boyhood vow. Joining the NAWCC. Meeting Mahlon. Repairing the Mini-Grandfather. My YouTube video. Judy Montana. Getting all the Allison clocks up and running. Laying the groundwork to find them a home in a museum.

My quest is winding down.

The **AMERICAN MYSTERY CLOCK**, circa 1943

If I explained how it worked, that would be telling!

PART FOUR
CONCLUSIONS

G

GREG'S STORY

(2022)

'I certainly have confidence in a man like you.'
—McCord Crandall, shop visitor

CHAPTER 36

November 2022

A random question from Mahlon brings something unexpected to the surface.

We've been reviewing Clocks Six and Seven—one is a round, desktop clock constructed entirely of Lucite; the other, a miniature steeple with four faces for four U.S. time zones. As usual, I capture Mahlon's comments on paper while he dissects the components—his culture doesn't allow me to video him.

He's chatty during these times; we've become friends over the course of three years. I'm five years older than he is—during one of our sessions I gave him an (unsolicited) opinion about his business and he referred to it as "big brother advice." I liked that.

"Very, very interesting," he mutters, staring through his loupe goggles at the interior of the steeple clock. "Charley, you are really inspiring me."

This second-person address doesn't surprise me. I've taken to propping up a photo of Charley above the workbench; Mahlon and I have gotten used to speaking to my grandfather as we work. We're a chummy trio.

Mahlon works to remove a tight screw. "Do you know if Charley had any apprentices?" he asks. Although I don't know it yet, this question is going to crack open the heart of my quest.

I run it through my mind. Along with the clocks, I have the box of pictures from Judy Montana. I've been through them a couple of times by now. There are many photos of my dad, his half-brother, my grandmother, and Charley—insight into my father's and grandfather's worlds that I haven't had previously.

More and more I've realized how much my father, as a boy, looks like young me. This has shaken me a little. The dad I knew was an overweight, sixty-year-old WWII veteran, frugal and frustrated with financial setbacks from the 1970s. He was prone to bouts of anger—sometimes throwing things (like bills, boundary maps; once a half-full plastic milk jug). I struggled to connect with him on any level. And yet, these photos prove that connection exists.

Young Darwin (1924) and Young Greg (1970)—cut from the same Allison cloth.

I consider Mahlon's question. Are there any photos of Grandpa with helpers? Whenever Charley is pictured with his clocks or in his workshop, it's just him.

"I don't think so," I reply, "I think he worked alone."

We move on to other topics but, once I'm in the car navigating the dark country roads home, my mind circles back to Charley and the prospect of an apprentice. A thought sifts up—something I realize has been percolating for months. Bringing it to the surface opens the floodgates.

Charley wasn't very close to his sons.

There it is, raw and exposed. I sit with it, feeling a sadness permeate the years.

Uncle Gordon lived near him in California, my left brain notes. *They must have had some kind of relationship.*

Yes, and Charley slammed him against the wall one time when he was angry, my right brain replies. *Plus Charley only saw Dad twice after the move from Rochester to Los Angeles. That must have hurt.*

It was a different time, Left Brain counters. *Cross-country travel was much more difficult back then.*

On the plus side, Jimmy Smith said Charley was good to him. Right Brain adds. *He called him 'Dad.' And many people wrote in the shop book about what a great friend Charley was. So he had some good to give, at least. And don't forget that he lost several siblings and a wife at a young age! That has to affect a person.*

What about Charley's own dad? Left Brain speculates. *We really don't know what it was like for him growing up with Frank. He might have struggled just like we did.*

Agreed, Right Brain concedes. *But, let's face it, that's still no excuse for inexcusable adult behavior.*

As with all things Grandpa, I don't have definitive answers, only clues to a complex man.

The night is clear. This far from city lights, the sky is speckled with stars. A nearly full moon accompanies me through the passenger window as I drive north. My thoughts continue to churn, as a more sensitive conundrum surfaces.

Would Charley like me?
Would I like him?
Would he be okay that I'm gay?
Would he have taught me his trade if I'd grown up at his knee?

Charley, the creative craftsman, may have struggled with his own sons, but he might have enjoyed an attentive grandson at his side. And I would have loved learning the mechanics of timekeeping—and maybe some of the mechanics of manhood. *Maybe I wouldn't have been afraid to ask him questions.*

I pass through the small town of Dansville and hop onto the expressway. Still an hour to go. The clear sky has made this November evening more crisp than it might have been beneath a thick layer of clouds. I turn the car's thermostat up a couple of degrees and let my mind continue to pick at the thread Mahlon's question has unraveled.

Charley wasn't very close to his sons…and my dad wasn't very close to me.

There it is—*more* raw, *more* exposed.

I struggled to know my father, Darwin, Charley's second son. He spent his own childhood in East Rochester in a smart-looking brick house that my grandfather built, just a twenty-minute drive from our own brick farmhouse. Dad pointed it out to me once when I was little.

"Look at those roof tiles," he said, gesturing through the windshield. "Those are original. Your grandfather used terracotta to last for a hundred years." I could hear the admiration in his voice at the craftsmanship of his father. The same guy who'd cheated on his mom and left for California when my dad was twelve.

Like most of the things I uncover in this search, there are elements of pride and moments of pain. But I'm old enough to recognize that this is probably true of most family stories—if you dig deep enough.

My father wasn't around very much when I was young, running his small grocery store during the work week and often playing the piano at restaurants on weekends. When he was around the house, it was almost always uncomfortable. As a kid, I never knew what would launch him into a verbal tirade.

His tantrums were mostly self-directed, anger at bureaucracy, or expenses, or Murphy's Law. I never felt physically threatened, so I didn't consider my childhood household abusive. (Years later, time on a counselor's couch forced me to reevaluate that).

I admire some things about my dad. He did family vacations up big—once renting a Winnebago to drive all eight of us to the Atlantic Ocean for a four-day, luxury-hotel, beach excursion. Earlier, when he built the mobile home park in the 1960s, he added his own creative flair, such as artistic streetlamps and a complex underground heating oil delivery system (that he'd designed).

With the advantage of fifty-six years of living, I can look back now and see that many (if not most) interactions with my father were transactional: help him take inventory at the store; drive papers to his accountant in the city; help survey a creekside lot he'd purchased.

The only times he sought emotional connection were while drinking—and conversations with Drinking Dad were excruciatingly long and, often, circular.

I think he was lonely for the company of men. He had drinking buddies who would occasionally stop by our house for a 'quick belt'—usually associated with small businesses or local politics. Many of our grocery store's male customers would tarry at the counter for morning coffee before going to their construction site, or manufacturing plant, or car repair shop. Dad would stand and 'shoot the bull' with them for what seemed like, to me, forever.

This camaraderie extended outside the bounds of our family, but seemed to stop at our front door. Looking back, it occurs to me that, maybe because we 'had to' love him, he didn't make efforts to nurture our relationship. Or maybe he was afraid of the intimacy that might have resulted. *Or lack thereof.*

As I've mentioned, Mom often made excuses. "Remember, his own father wasn't around," she'd say, whenever we grumbled about Dad's angry rants. "He doesn't know how to act." *From what I've uncovered about Charley, I'd say my father learned his fatherhood lessons well.*

I arrive home, kiss my husband, and eventually head to bed—but the thoughts Mahlon's question has ignited keep me awake for a long while.

'To an amazing artist.'
—Fibber McGee and Molly, radio comedians

CHAPTER 37

November 2022

The Wednesday before Thanksgiving, I am picking up pies at an East Rochester bakery. I've been toying with the idea of writing an article about my grandfather's watchmaking for the local East Rochester newspaper—if one still exists. After the pies are secured, I drive down Commercial Street and park at the center of town.

I know this territory well. Back in the '80s, I got my driver's permit from the Department of Motor Vehicles at the nearby mini mall. Back in the '90s, I was a systems administrator at a Xerox office inside the historic Eyer Building, right next to where I'm parked today. Beyond that, I haven't visited the heart of East Rochester in nearly twenty years.

Is there still a newspaper here?
Are there any records of Charley here?

It occurs to me that, after years of searching Los Angeles, I haven't looked around my grandfather's hometown—just fifteen minutes from my house. Sometimes I wonder what's wrong with me.

From the comfort of my heated car seat, I do a quick search on my phone. There doesn't seem to be a local newspaper anymore, but the public library has replaced the Xerox suites within the Eyer Building. Masking up, I head inside.

There are plastic Covid screens everywhere. Helpful signs point to restrooms, town offices, and a café. I find my way to the "Local History" section.

There's something about the ancient axiom 'a prophet isn't welcome in their own country' that has worked its way under my skin between the car and the library, although *prophet* and *welcome* aren't exactly the right words in my case. I'm not sure what words are.

Why have I neglected East Rochester in my search? Charley honed his craft here. Dad was born here. Charley built their family house here, breaking ground the day my father was born—it's just down the street.

An uncomfortable thought strikes me. *Am I like Dad? Do I try to meet my needs outside of my home circle—ignoring the things that are right under my nose?*

Maybe researching in Los Angeles is easier because it's so far away. If I look locally, there's baggage that comes with information.

For example, I know how proud my dad was that his father broke ground for the house on his birth date. As if to honor creation with creation. But the way Molly heard it from my grandmother was different. It was a bargain, a transaction. She'd give Charley a child; he'd build her a house. *And Charley actually wanted a daughter.*

Either my dad didn't know that—or he chose to gloss over it, the way I sometimes skirt past uncomfortable truths.

I've heard other things—ugly things—within family lore. That Charley was angry with my grandmother during the housebuilding—so he designed the place without closets, just to be spiteful in the launch of their family. That Charley was angry with my grandmother during their breakup—so he sold the house for less than it was worth, just to be spiteful in the divorce settlement.

This is the foundation I'm built on. Artistry and anger. Determination and disrespect. *How much of that have I inherited?*

In the Local History office, I encounter Anita, a talkative woman with glasses and a cane. "You came at a good time," she says. "We just wrapped up a meeting."

I shed my coat and sunglasses, taking in the room. It's a clean, orderly arrangement of crammed bookshelves and glass display cases. I give her the short version of my quest to locate my grandfather's clocks. "He built the brick house on the corner of Main Street and Fairport Road," I add.

Her eyes light up. Local history is clearly her swim lane. "I know that house!" she says. "It had a tile roof for a long, long time."

"Yes," I smile. "My grandfather built it to last." We briefly lament that the current owners replaced the tiles with shingles, sometime in the mid-2010s. *At least your roof made it to ninety, Grandpa.*

I spend the next hour with Anita. She talks about the demise of the local paper, just two years ago. I throw out dates of things I know about my father's and grandfather's lives. She brings me to a low bookshelf, adjacent to the conference table where we've been seated.

"We have high school yearbooks back to 1931," she points, then launches into the history of how the book was named after a Native American word, *gagashoan*, which means "storyteller." I'm only half listening, while my mind does the math from my dad's birth. He would have graduated high school in 1937 or 38. Both books are right in front of me.

While Anita continues about how proud she is that the Class of 2021 has devoted a whole page to the yearbook's naming legacy, I pull out the 1938 Gagashoan and thumb through the seniors. Nothing.

1937 next. I flip it open and, right there on the page, my young father is staring back at me *(with hair!)*. A paragraph of accomplishments and activities accompanies the photo. He worked on the yearbook. *Just like me.* He was in the Glee Club. *Also like me.* He was Chairman of the Committee for Student Affairs?

President of the Class? Wow.

I read his student quote. *But music for a time doth change his nature.* I know my dad started playing the piano in bars when he was fourteen—so that's a fit. But the rest of it—French Club, Dramatic Club, Library Club—is foreign to anything I've ever known about my father.

I wrap things up with Anita. Nothing about Charley has surfaced so, armed with her email address and promises to exchange more information, I head back to my car. I sit with the information I've gained about my dad, feeling a strange mix of emotions.

For years I've focused this quest on my grandfather, who I never had the chance to know. Learning unexpectedly about my father has been both exciting and unsettling. On the one hand, I love rounding out the story of my heritage. And yet—this new knowledge reminds me of one more ugly thing about my paternal lineage.

My father really didn't know me well…and I really didn't know him well either.

C

CHARLEY'S STORY

(1951 – 1955)

1951

Back in Rochester, Darwin married his girlfriend of six years, Betty, in September 1951. As a wedding gift, Charley and Margie shipped them a clear-glass clock. Upon receipt, Darwin called his dad, overjoyed to finally own one of his father's creations. Over the phone, Charley admitted the gift was not an Allison original—that he'd purchased it.

Sometime after that call, Charley packed up his latest creation, the Allison Mini-Grandfather, penned a short note: "SEE IF YOU CAN FIND ONE LIKE THIS! LOVE, DAD" and shipped it to his east-coast son.

Darwin opened the new gift and was so excited, he gave it a strong wind to bring it to life. Unfortunately, with no instructions, he wound it the wrong way (clockwise, instead of counterclockwise) and something inside snapped.

Darwin placed the broken clock on a shelf and sent a thank-you note to his father.

Charley and Darwin in 1923.
What lessons of manhood did my dad learn from his father?

1952

Life between Charley and Margie settled into a steady rhythm. Their living quarters in the back of the shop provided amply for their needs. They also had the cabin to retreat to—now a fifteen-minute drive away.

The new location continued to draw spectators to view the Allison Collection and sign the guest book. Entries in 1952 include references to Charley's latest (and what would turn out to be his final) creation: the Allison World Clock, standing just five inches tall.

With twelve miniature dials, each face named two cities at opposite ends of the globe. At a glance, an observer could track local time for any of 24 time zones around the world.

The Allison World Clock, pictured here against a global map in a professional photo shoot from 1952, stands just five inches tall.

1952

In addition to the Allison Mystery Clock, an even dozen timepieces now rounded out the Allison collection. Charley hired a professional photographer to shoot individual shots of his newest clocks, along with an overall view of the full display.

Ever the marketer, he used the photos to create promotional postcards of the World Clock, the Brass Torsion Pendulum Clock, and the entire Allison Timepiece Collection.

The Allison Timepiece Collection, on display at Allison Watchmakers.
Signage on the shelves reinforced that Charley's creations were NOT FOR SALE.

1955

On January 1, 1955, Darwin's second child, a daughter (Molly), was born. Darwin called his father to tell him the news—and family lore reports that Charley was, once again, overjoyed to be a grandfather to a granddaughter.

Perhaps this shared happiness gave Darwin the boost of confidence he needed. A few weeks later, he wrote to his father, explaining that the Mini-Grandfather had broken, and asked his dad for a repair.

He received a quick letter back from Margie, informing Darwin that Charley had suffered a brain hemorrhage—but that he would repair the clock once he recovered.

In January 1955, my grandfather suffered a cerebral event that left him impaired.

1955

Just weeks after Margie wrote Darwin about his dad's health issues, she called to say his father had taken a significant turn for the worse. Darwin caught a flight from Rochester to Los Angeles, but he did not arrive in time to see his father alive.

On February 26, 1955, Charles (Beale) Ernest Allison passed out of this world.

On March 4, Charley's remains were laid to rest at Glen Haven Memorial Park in Sylmar, CA.

In the weeks after Charley's death, Margie carefully wrapped each of his timepieces in cloth, gathered them into a box, and placed them in a closet.

There they would remain, untouched, for the next sixty-five years.

IN MEMORY
OF
CHARLES ALLISON

PASSED AWAY
FEBRUARY 26, 1955

INURNMENT
MARCH 4, 1955 11 A.M.
AT
GLEN HAVEN
MEMORIAL PARK

A Loving Memorial

The funeral program for my paternal grandfather, Charley Allison.

G

GREG'S STORY

(2022)

'You'll have the time of your life trying to figure it out.'
–Kendall Evans, shop visitor

CHAPTER 38

December 2022

A Saturday morning in early December, I run my latest musings past my writing group.

"Young Darwin seems an awful lot like the Greg I know," one friend states. "You two would have been best friends." She looks at me through the zoom screen, her eyes gentle. "What things in his life changed him into the man you knew?"

Another friend chimes in. "And, even deeper, you might want to explore: does Greg fear that he's like Darwin? Is Greg transactional in his relationships?"

A memory from 1997 surfaces, when I borrowed money from my parents for a down payment on my first house. I paid it back with 5% interest, which I was okay with—until, after my father's death, while helping my mom settle the estate, I learned that he'd made a similar loan to one of his tenants. The guy was around my age; it was around the same year. My father charged him 4% interest.

The familiar pattern: Dad treating people outside of our family better than us. Charley treating Jimmy Smith better than his own sons. I really don't think I'm like that.

The writing group zoom ends, but my friends' comments have stirred the primal pot that began bubbling a few weeks ago at Mahlon's. Honestly, I've heard similar feedback from a close friend who's read my manuscript-in-progress. "It seems like this story is more than just about finding clocks. I think we need to know what this search means to Greg."

I sit back in my chair for some necessary introspection. I glance at the clocks. Charley's spirit surrounds me. It's time for some conclusions.

It's easy for me to feel that I've inherited the best and avoided the worst from these men. However, I recognize that's not fair or honest. I'll never know if I might have repeated some of these behaviors—I'm not a father myself.

When I was a kid, I wrote in my journal about my desire to grow up and have six children, to emulate the good things I loved about our family (like singing around the piano, going as a group to midnight mass, laughing at our 'remember when' stories). Fate threw me a curve ball during adolescence when I figured out I was not attracted to girls. That's a long, lonely tale worthy of its own book.

Life, and then I, chose a different path. The man I eventually married was not interested in adopting children, something I knew up front. At thirty, I accepted that compromise.

The married men in my close circle (mostly high school friends and my older brother) have all become fathers, providing me with a pool of boy and girl relatives to assist in raising.

That said, I know that it's much easier to be Uncle Greg at their home for a day and then retreat to my own house at night. I've experienced some of the perks of parenthood with very little of the responsibilities.

I'm also very clear: I'm happy with my choice of husband and the life we've created together.

Which surprised me when, at forty-nine, I began to feel a gap—something that (loosely) translates to 'the loss of progeny unknown.' Whether this was simple vanity or the advent of male menopause, I'm still not sure. Either way, one frigid winter night (with a cosmo in hand), I fired up my laptop and began a search for 'sperm donation centers.' *Even if I can't be a dad, a part of me would continue somewhere. It could help a couple who is struggling to conceive.*

Over the next hour I learned that the closest 'repository' was in New York City, a six-hour drive away. Undaunted (and with a refreshed cosmo), I filled out the online application—including age, weight, and a brief health history.

In less than a week, I received a clinical email response. *Your application as a donor has been rejected.*

It should not have come as a surprise. As a middle-aged, overweight guy who lives 400 miles from the donation site—it's not rocket science to figure out I'm an incompatible candidate.

And yet, something about that rejection poked at my core. It dredged up feelings from my teenage years—feelings I thought I'd long-since processed through/accepted—about not being 'quite enough male' to be considered a man. *They don't even want my sperm.*

I related the story over lunch the next day (after we were done eating) to a close friend. We couldn't help laughing at the absurdity. When the giggling subsided, she said, very kindly, "I'm sorry your sperm got rejected."

That was seven years ago. More recently, during a Tampa visit, I was enjoying a beer with my thirty-year-old nephew, Joe. We were out for some 'guy time' just after I met his newborn son. The conversation naturally turned to parenting. I laughingly told him about my 'donor rejection.'

He got quiet for a moment, then spoke. "You would have been a good father. You were willing to get down on the floor and play games with us. And you were interested."

I know it's not the same as having a son—with all the joys and challenges—but, in that moment, those words meant everything.

Back at Mahlon's on a different Saturday, as we carefully pull apart another of my grandfather's clocks, I tell him about the themes in the book I'm writing. About getting to know Charley better and my struggle to know my father. "I will say this," I add, "at the end of his life, my dad became kind of a sweet old man. He told me lots of stories in those last couple of months. Mostly about his time in the war."

Mahlon smiles. "At least you had that nice ending," he says. My Amish friend is a glass-half-full kinda guy.

Being distant from my father is not a new revelation to me. But this is the first time I've connected the dots: this disconnect I feel might be something generational, something bigger than just me and my dad. In seeking Charley's world, I've been uncovering my dad—and, indirectly, myself.

For example, a few months ago, I was really irritated at my brother Mike (for being perpetually late). After I aired my grievances (somewhat emphatically) to him, he mentioned how much like Dad I was. The observation floored me (I've always thought *he* was the one most like our father).

I'm clear that I didn't inherit Charley's "mean streak"; I've never thrown anyone against a wall. I also don't think I've inherited Darwin's difficulties being emotionally close to the people I care about.

And yet.

The anger is there. The words from Charley's divorce decree haunt me: *[affiant claims defendant committed violent assault upon the person and body of affiant]*. I recall the day my father threw that box of spaghetti across his store. Sometimes I get so mad at my computer, I scream the foulest words I know and pound my desk. *Am I getting more like Dad as I age?*

The alcohol is there. I see photos of Charley with a whiskey tumbler in his hand. My dad was a prolific scotch drinker. Vodka is my go-to. Now in my fifties, I probably consume as much (if not more) alcohol than my own father—a guy I thought of as a borderline alcoholic. *Am I trying to bury the disappointments of older male life like I presume he tried to?*

The testosterone is there. Charley cheated on at least one of his four spouses. I believe my father was faithful to my mother but I recall, as a kid, snooping and finding a Hustler magazine in his nightstand drawer (he would have been right around my current age). And me? While my libido has diminished as I've passed the fifty-yard line, I'm certainly still in the game. The furnace still burns red hot sometimes, sometimes uncomfortably so. And the Internet is flooded with temptation.

In my mid-teens, I remember reading a Stephen King story about an older man (70s) talking to a younger man (30s). The former explained that, while he had

243

loved his now-deceased wife sincerely for their fifty years of marriage, he had also occasionally paid a woman in town to 'do things that he couldn't ask his wife to do.' That fictional conversation has stuck with me, all these years. *Who does a guy talk to about things that are impolite to discuss?*

Around the time I turned forty, I sought out a counselor to help me sort through some stresses in my life. I eventually found Dan, a straight guy, twenty years my senior. I met with him weekly for more than a year as we sifted through a strained sibling relationship, my weight issues, and a family medical crisis.

I remember one of our conversations about intimacy (non-sexual) among men. He related a story. "I remember being a kid with my dad in the locker room at the YMCA. All these pudgy, middle-aged guys walking around naked, just talking and joking. It felt so comfortable."

I laughed. "I actually have a similar memory," I said. "Although we ended up only going to the Y once."

Dan leaned in, like he always did when we got to the more important stuff. "Here's the thing. Just recently, after my heart attack, I joined the local Y. In the locker room, I was surprised to see so many guys with their towels wrapped tightly around their middles—all the time—like they were afraid to take them off, to relax, to be themselves." He sighed. "It made me sad. I think there's something lost there."

* * *

These memories tumble around me as I sit in my home office on a Sunday morning, surrounded by Charley's clocks. They greet me each day from their butcher block pedestal, ticking and spinning, carrying forward the craft of my heritage. They feel like his children to me, now in my care.

My friend's words echo in my head. *I think we need to know what this search means to Greg.*

The problem is, I'm not sure I've figured that out yet.

I feel the most close to an answer when I listen to that theme song I chose back in 2019. *Won't Give In* by the Finn Brothers. The lyric about what it means to be born with a name and then carry it on always grabs me.

I am an Allison. Is this what it is to be a man, a son, a grandson? To carry a name forward, with inherited behaviors for better and worse? To manage heart, mind, and soul, sometimes against the demands of a penis? To shine in some ways and struggle in others?

Outside my window, a winter snow has begun to fall—big, lake flakes that flood the air in their race to the ground. They match my mood, soft beauty against a dull gray sky.

How much of me is built in—and how much of it is within my control to change? What else is baked into my DNA—for good or bad—that will surface with age?

Three generations of young Allison men: Charley, Darwin, Greg.

At fifty-six, with my clock quest winding down, the search to know myself marches on. Like my musings about Charley, I haven't found specific answers to all of my questions about manhood. There are stereotypes and suggestions, but nothing definitive.

Leaning in, I have to admit that specific answers may not exist. I'm old enough to recognize that there isn't any one particular thing that makes a guy a man. We inherit male DNA (and, if fortunate, life lessons) from the men who have come before us. And then, as we age, we make choices about the men we want to be for the next generations. It's a different experience for each of us.

But…maybe that's okay. Maybe we don't need to box ourselves into a one-size-fits-all manhood equation. Maybe the willingness to keep searching for clues as sons, spouses, friends, fathers, uncles, grandfathers—maybe even *together*, in the locker room, or pub, or church, or basketball court, or wherever men choose gather in the future—might just, in itself, be enough.

Maybe the quest isn't meant to end.

EPILOGUE

Spring 2024

It's been a smoggy morning on this most recent visit to California. That said, as the day has progressed, sunshine has burned off the gloom. My car maneuvers the winding roads with ease, as cool afternoon air floods in through the open windows.

The street names on this final errand all have the word "canyon" in them, which probably accounts for the many curves. I slow for one—and a yellow "pedestrian crossing" sign crops up on my left. Except, instead of a stick-figure person, this one touts a horse-and-rider icon.

If this were a Hardy Boys mystery, Joe might be driving and Frank would offer some older brother caution as they rounded the bends (in their sporty jalopy). But, today, my imagination doesn't linger with the Hardys. Today is the opposite of mystery. Today, my path has definition and purpose.

Hills are everywhere, some in the distance, some hugging the road. Just when I'm convinced the air might be getting thinner, everything in front of me flattens out and, suddenly, I've arrived. Here's where the graves are.

I'm here for one final 'find' in this epic pursuit—one last gold nugget I can thank Judy Montana for. The location of my grandfather's grave.

It's curious to me how many cemetery records can be found online. These last years have taught me this much, as I've mucked through various sites with their click-bait ads, offering up discount plots and ancestry links. I'd struck out online trying to find Charley's final resting place. But the box from Judy Montana, my resourceful quest ally, has offered me one more gift.

We've spent some time together, the two Judys and I, since the original Jimmy Smith trip. Last summer, we gathered at the annual NAWCC convention, to man a booth displaying Charley's clocks and telling his story. Three days to chat, laugh, and bond.

"It was a really tough time when we were clearing out my dad's house," my stepcousin shared with me and my sister in between booth visitors. "My dad had told us to throw everything away, and my relatives had started the purge before I got there. At one point, I was sitting in the garage by myself, on a folding chair, feeling overwhelmed, staring at the trash bin."

A smile crept into her face. "Somehow, in that moment, I didn't feel alone anymore…it felt like there was an angel looking over my shoulder. I started picking through the papers in the bin. I realized they weren't just papers, they were photos, too. I recognized some of them as my grandmother and Charley…but a lot of the pictures had people I didn't know. People standing in snow.

"I realized they had to be photos of Charley's family from back east. And in the same breath, I knew that they were precious to someone—that we couldn't throw them out. That I had to try to find the east coast Allisons." She looked at me as her smile broadened.

"I know now the angel in the garage with me that day was Charley."

I smiled back and, in that moment, I could believe that Charley's spirit had guided her.

One of those rescued items is my treasure map today—the program from Charley's funeral, complete with cemetery name and burial date. Where the Internet has failed, a simple sheet of paper, folded into quarters, has succeeded.

When I discovered it months ago, I'd called the cemetery's office and learned two things. Yes, my grandfather was indeed buried there (*yeah!*) and no, there was no headstone (*what?*).

I'd wrestled with that for less than a day. It felt unsettling to know that his clocks could be celebrated in a museum while his remains lay beneath the dirt without notice. Dipping into my savings, I made the only decision that felt right.

I pull off the road and into the cemetery.

It's not large, Glen Haven Memorial Park, just a few acres of grass and trees with crisscrossed lanes. On the PDF map I've downloaded, it looks like a pie carved into wedges. Charley is in the right-hand slice.

I park next to the curb that says "Pinecrest" and sit for a minute. The moment feels charged, like the day my sister and I pulled into Judy Montana's driveway for the first time. Even moreso, given that Jimmy Smith has, himself, passed away peacefully at 92, just a year after our initial visit. It seems like I was meant to meet him, that last living connection to my grandfather.

A bird chirps somewhere from a nearby branch. I can't spot him, but his call sounds cheerful and sad all at once. I let out a sigh and open the car door.

There are graves everywhere—all flat stones, low to the ground, set at regular intervals across a long field. Nothing like the plot I've chosen for myself back home. My husband's and my grave is located in Rochester's oldest Victorian graveyard. There, walking paths curve up and down at random. My eternal landscape is peppered with gothic statues and noble mausoleums.

I orient myself with the map and begin to walk. Armed with a grid and numbers, it doesn't take long to locate the stone. They'd sent me a photo when it was placed weeks ago, but seeing it in person is different.

CHARLES E. ALLISON
May 13, 1892 – February 26, 1955
Watchmaker, Father, Grandfather

I stop and breathe.
I'm here.
He's here.
Me and Charley, the closest thing to a meeting that we'll ever have.

"Hi Grandpa, it's me, Greg," I say, as if he already knows me.
Maybe he does.
I snap a few photos with my phone.
"I wanted to let you know that I found your clocks. And that they're going to a museum, just like you wanted." After hearing my story, the National Watch and Clock Museum in Columbia, PA has offered to display the collection for a summer exhibit, with accompanying details about Charley and me both.
"We didn't find the big mystery clock," I add. "Jimmy's daughter thinks it probably got thrown out by mistake. But Mahlon and I figured out how it works, based on the smaller one you made. We're going to try to reproduce it sometime, based on pictures from your shop."

He probably knows all this already.
If he can know anything at all.
Is he here with me, watching my choices, guiding my steps?
How can I ever really know for sure?

I stand quiet then, trying to let whatever wants to come, come.
As I've said, these moments are hard for me. I want to be present and profound…and the calm part of me gets there. But the busy part of my brain continues its perpetual churn—currently wondering if I should set up my phone on a tripod and take video footage for that Ken Burns documentary.

Instead, I kneel near the grave and close my eyes.
Back near the car, the bird is still chirping. A faint smell of recently cut grass hits my nose. The tick of my wristwatch, barely audible, seems in sync with my heart, linking each beat to all those that have come before and all those that will follow.

A tumble of emotions tugs at me beneath my surface. Excitement at finding his grave. The lingering burden of his divorce decree. The pride in his creativity.
Thoughts tug as well. My father's link, my own link, to the bones beneath this ground. Turbulence and tenderness. The circle of life.

I open my eyes and take in the gentle hills, the azure sky, the splendor of the day.

"It doesn't look much like Rochester, Grandpa," I say, breaking the silence. A second thought surfaces. "But I think you found at least some happiness here."

"Your clocks are in my office with me every day," I continue, letting my mind go wherever it wants. "I wind them on Saturdays."

I think of the Mini-Grandfather back home, the clock that started me on this journey, its broken pendulum and the brokenness it had once captured between father and son. And, a generation removed, another father and son.

"I know now that you knew Dad broke your wedding gift," I tell the smooth stone in front of me. "It's fixed now. It runs great. I really wanted to let you know that."

A lone car speeds by in the distance. I hear its engine rushing to leave the cemetery in its wake.

"I guess I just wanted you to know that it's all okay now." I let the words come on their own, slipping out slowly, carefully. I feel my eyes moisten. "I'll take care of them now. I don't know if that means something to you, wherever you are."

My throat tightens. "But I want you to know that it means an awful lot to me."

I rest my fingertips on the carved letters of his name, my dad's name, my name.

ALLISON

"Goodbye, Grandpa. Maybe I'll see you sometime."

Straightening up, I brush the dirt from my knees and walk back to my car, ready for the long drive home.

APPENDIX
THE ALLISON COLLECTION
Observations by Mahlon Shetler, watchmaker

The Charles Allison Timepiece Collection

MINI-STEEPLE	PAPERWEIGHT	ART DECO	GREENWICH MEAN	BAKELITE TORSION	AMERICAN MYSTERY
1937 (estimated)	1938 (estimated)	1939 (estimated)	1940	1941	1943 (estimated)

ALPHA-OMEGA	POLE	COUPLES	BRASS TORSION	MINI-GRANDFATHER	WORLD
1944	1945 (estimated)	1946 (estimated)	1948 (estimated)	1950 (estimated)	1952

The Mini-Steeple Clock (1937, est.)
Full wind running time: 1 day

Covering the continental USA, Charley appears to have started out with a Waltham Model 1891, O size movement, ground all the engraving off and altered a wristwatch movement to fit into the bottom of the cylindrical tower case. The top has a standard style turret to drive the four dials.

It is my opinion that this is possibly his first, unless I see something more primitive from his collection. My reasons:

It is built using a very minimally altered movement. Although appearing complicated, it is not—it would be time-consuming to create.

Usual clocks like this would have four dials showing the same time. His shows the time in all four time zones, with the city 'painted' on the ledge. Later Charley built a real multiple time zone (12) clock, in which it appears he made nearly all the parts.

The clock shows considerable oxidation; demonstrating less knowledge on how to create a lasting finish.

Still, overall, a nice and desirable desk clock.

253

The Paperweight Clock (1938, est.)
Full wind running time: 3 days

This clock appears to be rather tame after looking at some of the other Allison clocks. Apparently, it was one of his first, if not the very first. One reason for this assumption is the fact that he used as his base movement a Waltham 8-day car clock movement, up-jeweled it, and made some alterations.

Note the Lucite screws, not only to secure the movement, but the case is also held together with what appear to be machined screws, almost assuredly made by Charley.

Did Charley have a connection to a Lucite salesman and this was used as a promotion? Or did he make this because he could?

The Art Deco Clock (1939, est.)
Full wind running time: 14.5 days

The art deco clock: it appears this could be one of Charley's earliest pieces. While it is finely machined and finished, the pallet fork and escape wheel are not quite as nicely finished as most of the pieces he made. Also, it appears he may have used a Waltham eight-day barrel and modified it.

Note the two brass screws and the two painted orange on the dial.

Note that Charley went to the trouble of finely finishing all cuts, ledges, and angles on the Lucite back cover.

It will be interesting to see if this piece runs for more than eight days.

(Author's note: it does—it runs for 14.5 days on one wind)

The Greenwich Mean Clock (1940)
Full wind running time: 9 days

The Greenwich mean time clock is one of the meanest clocks in Charley's collection. It was made of early plastic and, as usually happens, it shrank/contracted, capturing the movement plates. In the upper part, the bar across the middle held it from shrinking horizontally, but then all the shrinkage went into the vertical position.

After shaving off a few 100ths of a millimeter, we were able to extract the movement. As the photos show, the movement is rather basic in design—but it is notable that Charley used a red celluloid or plastic to make jewel settings—and they, too, shrank. They had previously been glued so as to stay put.

There are elements of finesse and less than finesse in this movement, a new discovery with a piece by Charley. You might say it appears he was having good and bad days. It appears he made most of the components in the main movement,

254

but used factory parts for some of the upper. For example, some of the screws used are identical to a Waltham 1892 plate screw—short head.

The Bakelite Torsion Pendulum Clock (1941)
Full wind running time: 730 days (est.)

The clear Lucite plates give the clock an interesting aura—if nothing else were to be unique about it. But there is. It has six ruby jewels (three each plate) for the last three arbors in the train. The clock most likely will run for more than one year, since there is an extra wheel and arbor, as compared to the usual 400-day clocks. And there appears to be ample power.

The clock appears to have a good finish throughout—and it appears Charley made nearly all components. The regulating system is unusual—but appears to be practical. The rotation of the brass disk throws the weights in or out, depending on the direction of rotation.

The clock is fitted with an extra-large escape wheel, compared to the norm—and has a pin pallet escapement versus the Graham escapement. The clock beats at 8 beats per minute.

The American Mystery Clock (1943, est.)

Author's note: If I explained how it worked, that would be telling!

The Alpha-Omega Clock (1944, est.)
Full wind running time: 16 days

One of the smallest clocks in the Charles Allison collection, but not the smallest problem. The case appears to be of aluminum, which reacted to the steel screws and the result was corrosion and locked screws. Plus, the back cover is celluloid, which caused further rust and corrosion, just like happens on a watch dial and hands with celluloid crystals.

After six weeks of soaking in Kroil, the back side screws had soaked enough to allow their removal (with much begging).

The mainspring barrel is decidedly a Waltham 37 size; the escapement is a wristwatch size, apparently made by Charley. Polishing pivots that are facing the celluloid was an absolute necessity. Otherwise the clock is good to run.

Charley was apparently just enjoying watchmaking—there is no special function, but still different.

The Pole Clock (1945, est.)
Full wind running time: 8 days

The clock on a pedestal/pole. Why the pole? It is the tube for the weight, which drives the balance escapement. A weight-driven balance escapement—I think it is a first for me.

It appears Charley made most of the plates using a partial train and escapement from a Waltham 8-day clock movement. This piece appears to be earlier, rather than later; note that there is very little adornment; all plates have a brush finish. It has 15 jewels.

The hands, indices, and the name are all made out of rosewood, as well as the base of the pedestal.

Getting the weight on the hook on the end of the cable—inside the tube—is challenging, and so it appears the clock must be transported with the weight on the 1/32 cable. Very carefully.

The Couples Clock (1946, est.)
Full wind running time: 11 days

This two-dialed clock with the dials at 90 degrees has two unique features. One is readily visible: the two dials. The other is not. It runs longer than eight days. A very small movement, the escapement being the size of a ladies watch (Bulova six series) powers this piece. It appears Charley made this because he could—and knew how difficult it would be for his contemporaries to copy him. One might say it is not so difficult—but this happened in the 1940s; a lot of technology was developed by then, but a lot more has happened since. Charley was a lone watchmaker, not part of a known guild, and certainly not part of a Peter Phillippe-style think tank. And this happened in America who, at the time, was losing out watch wise.

Take a look at the setup. A cannon pinion as usual, with a sidestepped drive shaft coming out to the turret. The design is very simple and effective. The winding and setting is operated from the bottom.

In short, a lot more details went into this clock than meets the eye on one glance.

The Brass Torsion Pendulum Clock (1948, est.)
Full wind running time: 730 days (est.)

Dual mainspring barrels, both driving the center wheel. Very clearly made escapement, admirably hand made. All plates perlaged on all sides, very finely finished throughout. The hands and indices are made of a flaming reddish Lucite, as is the case (black + translucent Lucite), with a glass front and side panels. In all the thousands of torsion pendulum clocks I have seen, there is no equal to this one. It has the fine escapement of an Atmos, but has a double mainspring. Tradition has that it runs two years on a winding. I would believe this to be possible in part because the push was to make long running clocks—the Atmos was still under development to become what is as we know it today.

The Mini-Grandfather (1950, est.)
Full wind running time: 8 days

When I first looked at the Allison miniature grandfather clock, I was reasonably sure the chime tubes were faux, but I was not so sure about the pendulum. I had seen numerous miniature clocks showing a pendulum but, so far as I can recall, they were all inanimate. Admittedly, I thought that would be the case here—until the back was removed and I was able to see the counterweight behind the main plate.

The balance wheel was the obvious timekeeper. My question: How did the train kick the pendulum to keep it going? That answer was revealed upon further disassembly—the spring wires and the 15-point star wheel inside the pendulum counterweight.

It was immediately apparent that the mainspring barrel and second wheel were from a Waltham car clock, but the winding arbor appeared to have been made in-house; the ratchet wheel being integral to the arbor. It is quite possible that the escapement may have been sourced from Switzerland, or even borrowed from an existing watch—but I believe all plates to have been designed and machined in-house, and quite possibly parts of the train, the blued screws, the case, the hands, etc.

After the broken gear was repaired and the clocked was reassembled and given a slight amount of power, the pendulum started swinging slowly—even while held in a horizontal position—resembling that of a full-size grandfather clock.

The World Clock (1952)
Full wind running time: 12 days

There is less to write about this clock even though I am more excited about it. The photos show most of the details. It appears Charley's made most of the components. Note the screws are made in a very fine manner, but not all alike.

The escapement appears to be made by Charley, as well as all the other components of the actual movement. As usual, he would most likely have purchased the jewels.

ACKNOWLEDGMENTS

This book is the culmination of a long journey, with many intersections. I'm truly grateful for support on multiple fronts including:

For the NAWCC Chapter 13 (local), especially Ed Olesky, Laurie Kimble, and Frank Ziefel, whose willing assistance pointed me south to Amish country. For the NAWCC (national), especially Cathy Gorton, Laura Taylor, and Rory McEvoy, whose interest in this project has granted a posthumous gift to my grandfather in the form of a museum exhibit.

For Eric Wilder, one of the most creative guys (and cover designers) I know.

For my writing group friends, including Paul Dingman, Judy Fuller, Erin Green, Sonja Livingston, Jenny Lloyd, Lee McAvoy, and Elizabeth Osta, whose gentle feedback and encouragement walked with me on every chapter. And for Jim Grimsley, who provided a full book critique (including some solid advice on restructuring).

For Beth Muller, for her enduring quest companionship and her full-read, thematic-thread suggestions.

For John and Janelle Shaughnessy, for putting me up during (and putting up with) my west coast questing.

For George Fogelson, who performed research for the price of a lunch, just because he's a really nice guy.

For my sister, Judy Allison of Florida, who's always ready to step onto a plane and support me in whatever crazy dream I'm pursing.

For my husband, Jeff Denmark, who read the final draft and (with the assistance of his discerning red pen), gave me helpful editorial direction.

For Mahlon Shetler, who won't want me to praise his excellent craftsmanship and ingenuity (which, in my opinion, parallels my grandfather's), so I will simply say that, without his sincere willingness to dive into this project headfirst, and his skill at getting into the mind and heart of my grandfather, I could not have brought this quest to closure. Without question.

For my newfound Montana family, including Judy Allison and Jimmy Smith, whose generosity gave this tale a most happy ending indeed.

For my father, Darwin Bryan Allison, who must have struggled more than I ever appreciated.

And, finally, for my grandfather, Charles Beale Ernest Allison, whose complicated life and creative legacy have influenced the man I am today.

This one's for you, Grandpa.

ABOUT THE AUTHOR

Gregory Gerard Allison's work has been published by *Tiny Lights*, *Jonathan*, *Lake Affect*, and other journals. He is the author of *In Jupiter's Shadow* and *The Traveling Suit*, as well as editor of *The Big Brick Review*.

Gregory resides in Rochester, New York, with his husband of 24 years. For more details on his writing, visit GregoryGerard.net. To learn more about his grandfather's collection, visit CharlesAllisonClocks.com.

Photo by Sonja Livingston

Rest in peace, Jimmy Smith.
1931 - 2023

Cousins and clocks, united by a shared quest, September 2022.
L-R: Judy Allison (Montana), Jimmy Smith, Judy Allison (Florida), Greg Allison.

www.ingramcontent.com/pod-product-compliance
Lightning Source LLC
Chambersburg PA
CBHW070100030426
42335CB00016B/1960